Nuggets

of

Wisdom

II

CW01431733

Learning & Sharing

in

Shorthand

Also written by

Elsie Spittle

Wisdom for Life

Our True Identity...Three Principles

Beyond Imagination - A New Reality Awaits

Nuggets of Wisdom - Learning to See Them

The Path to Contentment

Nuggets of Wisdom II

Learning & Sharing in Shorthand

Elsie Spittle

Nuggets of Wisdom II
Learning & Sharing in Shorthand
by Elsie Spittle

Copyright © 2020 Elsie Spittle
www.3phd.net

ISBN 9798670599771

Published by Amazon Kindle Direct Publishing

All rights reserved. No part of this work covered by the copyrights hereon may be reproduced or used in any form or by any means—graphic, electronic or mechanical—without the prior written permission of the author, except for reviewers who may quote brief passages. Any request for photocopying, recording, taping or storage on information retrieval systems of any part of this work shall be directed in writing to the author.

First printed in 2020
Printed in the USA

Editor: Jane Tucker
Cover design and book layout: Lynn Spittle and Kim Patriquin
Author photo: Lynn Spittle
Cover photo: Andrew Dyer Photography
www.facebook.com/andrewdyerphotography

Note: All client names are fictitious

About the Author

Elsie Spittle was a personal friend of Sydney Banks before he had his epiphany. After initial resistance, she realized the profundity of Syd's discoveries and was the first person to formally share them with the public and mental health professionals.

Elsie went from life as a homemaker to becoming a global consultant and mentor of leading Three Principles practitioners, devoting her life to sharing this transformative mental health paradigm with the world.

She had the privilege of receiving "on the job" training directly from Mr. Banks, travelling with him to address mental health practitioners, educators, and others seeking a deeper understanding of life.

Elsie Spittle is highly regarded as a public speaker because of her ability to reach an audience, large or small, via a "feeling" that touches the heart and soul.

Married for 57 years, with a loving and supportive family, she has her own private business and is co-founder of the Three Principles School, located on Salt Spring Island, BC.

This is Elsie's sixth published book.

Elsie's website: www.3phd.net

Endorsements

What people are saying about Nuggets of Wisdom II:

"There is a line in *Nuggets of Wisdom II* that epitomises the content of the whole, as well as touching on what Elsie Spittle's writing is so evocative of: 'simplicity versus complexity, of stillness versus noise, of love versus ego.' In this selection of insights, you will be invited to turn your own gaze inwards in order to realise the simplicity, stillness and love that reside there, ever present, and in service of humankind."

Dr Giles P Croft, former NHS surgeon, writer, speaker and Three Principles practitioner.

"Elsie Spittle is a mentor, a unique teacher, a human relations consultant and a student of the teachings of her dear friend Sydney Banks. She has already published six books and in this, her latest one, *Nuggets of Wisdom II*, she gives her readers an even more intimate and insightful experience that comes from her own spiritual evolution journey.

The fact that this book is shared in 'shorthand' makes it rich and real; it has touched a deep place in my heart. Thank you, Elsie, for your honesty, for that integrity coming from your soul!"

Ana Holmback – Entrepreneur, Child Advocate, and podcast host of "The Relevance of Sydney Banks' Role."

"My experience of Elsie is like being bathed in love. She embodies The Principles and gently points me back to my essence. The truth and deep feeling within *Nuggets of Wisdom II*, prompted the gentle exhale that accompanies wisdom and insight. I touched the stillness of my soul. I remembered that I am always home. Thank you, Elsie."

Claire Shutes is a Master Transformative Coach and Three Principles Practitioner. Founder of Potent Coaching in 2006, Clare has an international client base.

"Respectful applause for the words of Elsie Spittle in her book, *Nuggets of Wisdom II*. With humble grace, her words point to the wisdom and spiritual essence of all life, our human birthright. As Elsie suggests, this book is one to read slowly, savoring and feeling each 'nugget' offered. I highly recommend this book to anyone who wants to see, hear and feel beyond the thought stories that so often master our lives. This book will point you home. Chin'an – thank you, Elsie, for your enduring offerings to the world."

Karen E. Evanoff, academically trained in Cultural Anthropology and Human Services. Life training, in documentation to preserve the ancient wisdom of Indigenous people – remnants of what this book points to.

"Elsie's writing, where her words come from and where they point to, is a treasure for humankind. Profoundly simple and magically beautiful, it's impossible for a reader's soul to not be touched, re-awakened and nourished. Every paragraph seems to quieten my own mind, reminding me of who I really am; leaving me with a strong and a certain peace. Blending Elsie's own insights and recollections of her life, loves and travels, this book reminds me of the everyday miracles in my own life. *Nuggets of Wisdom II* is a true gift to the deepest part of ourselves."

Wyn Morgan, Founder and CEO of Wynning Coaching and Training

This is what people had to say about Elsie's previous books:

"If my experience of reading *The Path to Contentment* is any indication of how others will feel, then Elsie Spittle has just made a major contribution to the field of mental health by helping people more deeply appreciate their own innate health and well-being. As I see it, this appreciation is exactly what Syd Banks had in mind when he stated that the Three Principles would fundamentally change the fields of Psychology and Psychiatry. Thank you, Elsie!"

Robert J. Solomon, MD, adult, child and adolescent psychiatrist in private practice.

"Elsie Spittle's book *The Path to Contentment* is Soul Music. It is a gentle, honest and insightful sharing of the understanding of the Three Principles and our True Nature. As I read each chapter, I felt incredible peace of mind and felt warm feelings of love and understanding rise to the surface.

As a psychologist, I know that the principles shared in this book offer hope for humanity to find the well-being they are searching for; hope that people can transcend their emotional problems, addictions, and relationship difficulties to discover the love, understanding, and wisdom that insights into the principles uncover."

Mark Howard, PhD, is recognized as one of the original professionals bringing this understanding to psychology and related fields. In 2008, Mark was granted the "Outstanding Career Service" award by the Santa Clara Psychological Association for his Three Principles work.

"Elsie Spittle is a treasure—warm and wise with a depth of understanding that illuminates human psychology. In her book, *Nuggets of Wisdom*, she shares hundreds of discreet invitations to awaken to our own ultimate resource—the wealth of wisdom within us."

Michael Neill, radio show host and bestselling author of The Inside-Out Revolution.

"*In Beyond Imagination* Elsie Spittle shares her improbable journey from housewife to international consultant. Elsie's sharing of the Three Universal Principles, as revealed to her friend Sydney Banks, is done with clarity, warmth, elegance and ease.

Reading this book will awaken many souls to their 'true identity' and an experience of peace. From that perspective, Elsie's vision of world peace looks not only possible, but likely."

William F. Pettit Jr. MD, Co-owner Three Principles Intervention LLC; Former Associate Professor of Psychiatry, West Virginia University School of Medicine.

"In *Our True Identity* Elsie described her first meetings with Sydney Banks, her initial reactions, and how she finally realized the truth behind what he was saying. Elsie draws the reader into an extraordinary story—told in a wonderfully ordinary fashion. Once the reader is quite comfortable, Elsie begins giving actual examples of people who are finding insights from within their own wisdom. This touched me deeply. These stories remind us that beautiful feelings and peace of mind are not dependent on time or circumstances; they do, indeed, exist before time. To the author, I want to say, 'Thank you, thank you, thank you, for writing this book.'"

Gordon Trockman, MD, Psychiatrist.

.

Dedication

To my husband, Ken:

I couldn't have traveled this journey without your consistent love and support. In the early years, when I was away on consulting trips or speaking engagements, you were the caregiver for our children. You did this without question, knowing I was doing my part in helping share Syd's message. I'm forever grateful for that and for our deepening love and tenderness.

To my children, Ron and Lynn:

You've been with me on this life long journey, often times wondering what on earth was going on with Mama! Yet you've always supported me, with love. When you were youngsters, and Uncle Syd would come visiting, you always loved having him in our home. And as you became adults, you began to get a glimmer of Uncle Syd's vision of hope for the world. You contributed to this vision; simply by living your lives as best you could. I thank you for that, from the bottom of my heart.

And deep appreciation for Lori and Kim, spouses of Ron and Lynn. Thank you for sticking with me, through thick and thin.

My eternal gratitude to Sydney Banks, Scottish mystic and visionary extraordinaire.

Author's Note

These "nuggets" are offered as they came to me in the moment, grouped by topic rather than in chronological order, and as such, are often related in the present tense.

I suggest you read them leisurely, as you would listen to music, without anything on your mind. Listen softly, hold the words lightly, and let your soul shine with the light of understanding.

Contents

Introduction

It's been my privilege to share the Three Principles understanding since 1974. In that time, I've experienced many different phases of spiritual and mental evolution, which moved me from an unhappy, depressed wife, mother, and homemaker to a happy, content, and fulfilled woman, who has become a global consultant. It's not been an easy journey. There have been times when I wanted to give up, especially in the early days, when Sydney Banks' teachings didn't make sense to me. I often felt like I was being pulled through a knot hole, my intellect fighting my true nature.

The beauty of this understanding is that it doesn't need to make sense in order for us to benefit from it. How can that be? This process seems to be mysterious and magical—yet the natural wisdom that resides within each and every person rises to the occasion despite disbelief, anger, and fear. I know. I experienced each of those feelings and more during my eighteen months of resistance to Syd's teachings.

The penny finally dropped, after what I felt was my last encounter with Syd. I was in a terrible mood, feeling like life was not worth living, when I saw Syd and his late wife, Barb, driving up our driveway. Some of you may know that Syd and my husband, Ken, worked together for a number of years at a pulp mill, before Syd has his profound enlightenment in 1973. Ken introduced me to Syd and Barb one afternoon and soon the four of us became fast friends. We enjoyed being together and talking about what was wrong with the world, with the union, with management of the mill. We were in alignment in our "what's wrong" reality. Seldom did we talk about what was right. Yet we enjoyed our time together. We enjoyed our insecurity, although if you would have suggested to any one of us that we might be harboring insecure thoughts, given our "what's wrong" world, we would have adamantly denied it. We simply thought we knew best. . . .

It's amazing to me now, when I look back at that time, how innocently lost we were. Then out of the blue, Syd had this brief, extraordinarily powerful insight where he experienced his true nature, God. Three days after this, he and Barb came to visit us. As soon as I saw him, I could see that something was different about him. He looked so at peace, filled with light, years gone from his face and body.

He shared what he'd learned during those brief spiritual moments of being enveloped in God. He said he'd found the secret to life. He told us that the spiritual gifts he'd uncovered had the power to change the fields of psychology and psychiatry. He shared that he now knew what God was, and he looked at me directly, with the utmost love in his eyes, and said, *"God is not what you think it is, Elsie."*

Those words went right to my soul, then moved to my intellect, and I froze. To say I was stunned is an under-statement, and as I looked at Ken, I could see that he also was feeling at a loss.

Nuggets of Wisdom II

Syd confided that he and Barb would be travelling the world sharing these spiritual gifts, and he said to us, *"If you hear what I'm saying, you will also travel the world and share these gifts."*

That was far too much for me to comprehend; after all Syd was a welder at the time. How on earth did he think he was going to be accepted by the world as having the "secret to life"?

As Ken and I felt more and more uncomfortable in Syd's presence during that first visit, Syd gracefully left us on our own, and drove off with Barb. As soon as they were out the door, Ken and I began to talk about what had just occurred. We finally came to the conclusion that Syd may have been having a nervous breakdown. Yet he looked so at peace, so filled with light; how could he be having a breakdown? A thought crossed my mind, that if this is what a breakdown looks like, I wouldn't mind having one as well.

Our visits with the Banks' continued. We truly enjoyed their company and were very aware of how their relationship had changed from an insecure one to one where they seemed to have fallen in love again, after fourteen years of marriage. I was very puzzled and curious about how that could happen, yet my fear also was increasing, so I was clear with Syd that we'd love to be with them, on condition they didn't talk about "this nonsense"...

Elsie Spittle

One day when I noticed them coming up our driveway, in my angst, I couldn't bear to see them. I hid in the bathroom, the only safe place in our open concept home. Long story short, when I heard the front door open, and Syd calling my name, I remained silent, my arms around myself, as if protecting me from harm. Then after a few moments, I heard the door close. To this day, it astonishes me how something propelled me out of my hiding place like a shot, and I went to the door to invite them back.

Syd immediately noticed my angst and put his arm around me to comfort me, saying, *"You'll be okay, dearie. You have God within you, as does every person on this planet."*

That declaration was far too much for me, and I hastily opened the door for them to leave. I was filled with fear at his statement. As they drove off, Barb said to Syd, *"I guess that's it for our friendship with Elsie and Ken."* Syd's response was, *"No, Elsie heard something today."* Barb said in disbelief, *"She sure has a funny way of showing it. She showed us the door!"*

Shortly after they left, I had another conversation with a mutual friend, and after hanging up on my friend, who was not agreeing with me as she usually did, about what nonsense Syd was spouting, I had a profound shift in my understanding. It was like the doors to true knowledge opened within me. In the midst of my anger, I had my first insight; Thought creates feeling. My inner evolution had begun, and I was moved by an overwhelming feeling of relief. I wept with joy, and for the first time, I felt worthy. I learned that the power of insight can pierce our fear, anger, and disbelief. Insight is like magic. It shows us what is rather than what isn't.

After 46 years of sharing this precious gift of true knowledge, Mind is guiding me to a simpler life, one with less travel and less public speaking engagements. As my mind is getting quieter and clearer, I'm learning to share and speak in "shorthand." More insights are coming to me, without doing anything except cherishing the stillness of my mind, part of Mind.

I offer this book, filled with insights from myself, and from clients. I hope you enjoy, and that this book prompts insights from within yourself. After all, you, the reader, are your best friend, and your personal mentor. The wisdom within is our spiritual birthright. Enjoy that gift. Cherish that gift. It is ours to create a world of beauty, love, and understanding.

We Are the Principles

We Are the Principles

I love the simplicity of Sydney Banks explanation: *"Mind, Consciousness, and Thought are spiritual gifts that enable us to see creation and guide us through life"*.

⁓

Universal Mind is the spiritual creative energy of all things, both form and formless. Consciousness is our awareness of who and what we are, at a core level. An awareness that we are spiritual beings having a human experience. We are blessed to use the gift of this spiritual energy to create our experience in life, via the power of Thought. We are the Principles in motion.

⁓

When I realized that every insight is a result of the 3 Principles working as One, my understanding took a huge leap. Each insight involves all 3 Principles; Thought articulates the insight, Consciousness provides the awareness of insight, and Mind is where the insight comes from. I never fully realized this before. I'm astonished and humbled. How can something so simple be so hidden? A mystery to the intellect is obvious to wisdom.

Elsie Spittle

I feel honored and excited about my session at the May 2017 3PUK conference, entitled The Three Principles in Faith and Religion, with Rabbi Shaul Rosenblatt and Mamoon. To share the stage with a Rabbi and Imam, as a non-practicing Catholic, and talk about how our understanding has shifted since being introduced to the Three Principles, was a privilege. It was an experience of three speaking as One. Each of us, from such diverse backgrounds, speaking One truth—going deep into the feeling of Mind, a journey into the simple truth behind life.

⁓

Ultimately, the Three Principles understanding is simply a platform to a more profound experience. The goal is to point us towards something deeper and more fundamental within ourselves.

⁓

After a conversation with a new friend, I was struck again by how much the Principles are a part of us, whether we know it or not, whether we want this to be so or not. We don't have a choice about living in the world of gravity; it just is. It's the same with the Principles—they just are. We are the Principles in action—so it makes sense that we want to learn about this wonderful gift and share all the implications this knowledge has for us and for the world.

Nuggets of Wisdom II

Instead of 'seeing' that our thinking is creating our stress/anxiety/messed up relationships—consider another way, a way of 'seeing' that we are the Principles. In the phrase: "I—See—Thought," "I" = Mind, "See" = Consciousness, "Thought"= Create. We use the Principles in unison to create our experience in life.

———

I want to share this beautiful comment regarding the "I—See—Thought" chapter in my book, *The Path to Contentment.*

"Hey Elsie, thank you for this post. When I read this line in your book: "While I was concentrating on achieving more, whether work, money, better life, I wasn't truly being in service, to myself, or to the world," something hit me right in between my eyes (it was a literal sensation). I felt so much pain around my eyes and started crying profusely. My eyes have been focusing on what's lacking, what's missing, what's going wrong all this while. I have eyes to see but I don't focus on seeing what's already going well. Your post has touched me so deeply, thank you."

Elsie Spittle

Another comment on "I—See—Thought": "This, in its simplicity, in its truth, just this – brought tears to my eyes and I wish that the entire world could see thought, if only for an instant, and in that instant experience the truth that we are. Thank you."

⁓

When our minds are entrenched in long held beliefs, it's hard to change. I know it was difficult for me when I was first introduced to this understanding. I wanted to live in the feeling that Syd did, but I didn't want to look at myself with honesty. I thought my lot in life was a result of my circumstances, not the way I used the Principles, innocently, against myself. I remember Barb Banks asking me during my early resistance, if I was happy. I indignantly replied, "Of course." She smiled, and said nothing more. However, her question hit my soul, and I listened, and changed.

⁓

When I first started to learn about the Principles, I didn't realize they were "neutral." Frankly, I didn't have a clue what the Principles did or what they were. When I realized the role of Thought in creating our moment to moment experience, I could finally "see" the connection between thought and feeling. Still, I didn't realize the neutrality of the Principles. They seemed more an entity to me rather than the formless energy behind life.

———

As I continued to evolve in my understanding, I saw with more clarity that the Principles are a powerful force, a spiritual, formless energy that takes on shape according to our thinking. Awareness of this inner process, Consciousness, automatically strengthens the connection between the human being and the spiritual being. Mind, the creative spiritual intelligence behind life, helps us to understand, via insight, how formless energy takes shape through our usage of Mind, Consciousness, and Thought.

———

In the early days of my spiritual evolution I believed that the Principles and wisdom were more esoteric than practical. Even though I'd had one insight that showed me the "truth" of our true nature, I still wandered off the path into questioning how inherent our wisdom was. Delivering philosophic statements sounded wise but I didn't think their sentiments were necessarily "practical."

Now, I see our inner wisdom as very practical, the very essence of Mind guiding us in our everyday lives. There's nothing the

Principles aren't part of; they have the power to take us "home" to our spiritual core. When we feel bereft or lost because of an impending challenge, we can rest more easily, knowing we have a safety net under us, protecting us even when we fall into our troubled thoughts. Somehow, the "feeling" of the safety net provides us with solace and comfort. From that spiritual space, answers and solutions do arrive.

It seems to me there are two essential elements to help us on our inner evolution: know that we are the Principles in motion, and know that the feeling of well-being is the vehicle for change.

Sometimes we look to others in relationships to feel "complete." Know that when we uncover our true nature, we are complete, because we are the Principles. And the Principles are the complete package.

Beyond "possibility" and "potential" there is certainty in who we really are on the inside; focus on what is rather than what isn't.

Nuggets of Wisdom II

Someone asked me if an atheist can believe/live in the Principles. This is my response: yes, an atheist can believe in the 3Ps. Anyone can because that's who we are; the Principles in action.

The Principles are formless energy, that some call God. The energy is neutral, and when we feel that deep energy within, we are moved beyond "belief" to "knowing."

The feeling we want people to get is a feeling of "knowing" who they are on the inside, not striving with their intellect to continue searching. "Be still and know that I am God" is a famous saying and so true.

I know that not everyone is comfortable with the words "spiritual" or "God" so in that case, we're back to fanning the flame of deep feeling emanating from within, which produces insight that answers the questions.

Elsie Spittle

This is from a grateful woman: "I just wanted to let you know that after the webinar where you spoke about trusting our wisdom more, the classes I gave went beautifully. I trusted my wisdom deeply as you reminded us, and it was just wonderful to experience. When participants came back for the third class their faces were smoother, less lined, glowing, I don't even think they realized it; it was beautiful to witness. Classes ended last week but I saw three of the participants yesterday and their faces still looked so smooth, relieved, so beautiful. It brings me to tears just thinking of it, reminds me of the deep relief the Principles offered me when I first 'heard' them."

May 2017: a wonderful 3P UK conference! Well done to the whole team who put their hearts and souls into organising this epic event. Extraordinary response to the simplicity of deepening our understanding. People clearly are resonating with the universal truth that they already have wisdom within them, just waiting to be released. People are realizing the ease and joy of continuing to deepen our understanding of the Principles by realizing the simplicity factor. Why are people resonating so deeply? Because we know in our souls that we're already what we're looking for!

Nuggets of Wisdom II

I love that we don't have to understand the Principles in order to "feel" them. When we feel them, this means we have a degree of knowing—not belief—but knowing. When Syd Banks told me this, my life changed from being anxious, because I didn't understand the Principles, to "feeling" blessed that it didn't matter. I did the dance of joy!

This is what I'm discovering. Relaxing into your true Self is how the Principles become more visible. Simple. Enjoy!

As the gap lessens between our spiritual nature and human nature, we feel more complete, more in balance. The bridge crossing the gap is our understanding of the 3 Principles; that we are the Principles in action—that we are One.

If we're waiting for someone to help us find peace of mind, we're giving away our spiritual power. Only we can find peace of mind within, regardless of our circumstances.

Mind

Mind

I used to think that the personal mind was separate from Mind. When I "heard" the following quote that appears in Syd's book, *The Missing Link*, it made a huge difference for me. It simplified my understanding. This gave me more faith, inner strength and calmness.

"An important thing to realize is that Universal Mind and personal mind are not two minds thinking differently, but two ways of using the same mind."

Universal Mind is the source of both form and formlessness. It draws us inward; It is us, and we are It. The more we realize that, the less duality there is.

It's not always easy to listen to Mind. Sometimes personal thinking is so compelling. When we do listen, Mind takes care of us and good things come our way.

15

A wonderful way to live—when we honor Mind, Mind honors us, and continues to shine the light on our unfolding path.

⤳

A client helped me see that volume isn't about the number of people we reach; it's about the volume of Mind essence that is released when we let that energy loose from within ourselves. That living energy is the "teacher."

⤳

Our life will never be totally smooth and unruffled. Mind provides us with the opportunity to learn. Don't wait for a perfect life before you share those feeling of peace and great joy.

⤳

Insights come from our innate wisdom, Mind in motion. Nothing to do—just be open to this spiritual fact.

⤳

When we doubt our wisdom, thinking "we could do better," we're disrespecting Mind, where wisdom comes from. This keeps us stuck in our ego/intellect. Let's free our Mind and let it fly!

Someone asked me about the different meaning I put to "I" and "inside". He said, "Many of us relate to "I" as our thoughts about ourselves." This is how I see it: When I talk about "I" being Mind, I'm not talking about the personal "I". I'm talking about the Universal "I" which is our spiritual being.

After spending four wonderful days mentoring a beautiful soul, I'm feeling spiritually full and empty at the same time; unexplainable mystery of Mind. Feels like the "allness" and the "isness" that Syd referred to.

Form and Formless

Often times, clients will ask me about the Oneness, telling me they find this topic confusing. Me too! When I try and figure it out intellectually, I find it very confusing. Then I'm reminded of Syd telling me years ago, *"Don't listen to my words. Listen to the feeling!"*

The Oneness is a deep feeling of connection, of harmony, of form and formless being One; the essence from which life and all the physical world is formed. I have a sense of the Oneness of our human and our spiritual nature, of soul connection with humanity. I have love and deep respect for nature and all of God's creatures. When we experience the feeling of Oneness, form and formless in harmonious accord, this is Truth in motion. This is what is, not what isn't.

Oneness is soul to soul connection, our true nature listening and speaking to one another. Sometimes I feel that we look to philosophical answers and tend to dismiss the practicality and common sense of the Oneness, the connection that we experience in our relationships and conversations. We innocently minimize what is most important: Oneness/connection.

⌒

Because form and formless are One essence, answering an intellectual question from the feeling of wisdom will quiet the intellect and provide an opening to hear Self.

⌒

The old adage "less is more" continues to unfold. It shows up as "less form—more feeling." The depth of feeling experienced when there is less form, less explanation of how the Principles work, illustrates how wisdom truly does the "work" for us, in the moment. That deep feeling of connection awakens the inner consciousness, the soul of whomever we come into contact with. Such ease and simplicity; such wonder in this spiritual unfolding of humanity.

⌒

Although we are an infinitesimal part of formless energy, the word "infinite" is contained in "infinitesimal". This tells me that we have infinite potential. Now that is awesome!

Elsie Spittle

Build your business by embracing your true nature. The depth of feeling that is released when this happens will draw people to you. This is building via the formless versus building via the form. Both work—you decide which may be less effortful.

I learned that when I have too much form or product in sharing the Principles, it's like a buffet of empty calories. Being present in the moment is what connects and draws out the wisdom of others.

Quiet Mind

The feeling at this session of the Three Principles School on Salt Spring Island was rich with deep insights from participants and times of stillness together in perfect harmony. No words were necessary. The silence was the educator and prompted many insights; a sacred space held and cherished in this gathering. What a privilege to see how Sydney Banks' message, that we're all the same spiritual energy, bonded us together, sending a ripple of pure love into the world, providing comfort to those in need.

I feel like I've got a new appreciation for "'time off"; having a quiet mind and just "being in the moment" is providing space to enjoy my surroundings like never before.

Slowing down allowed music into my soul. . .a wonderful experience of being serenaded. New insights began to emerge as my mind stilled; how to be in service without losing myself in the busy world of form. "Listen to that inner music" is what wisdom told me.

Elsie Spittle

Finding independence from our thinking leaves space for a quiet mind where insights are born and grace resides. When we get quiet inside, the feeling of calm has the power to still others so they can hear their wisdom.

One becomes "super conscious" the more our personal mind is stilled, freeing mental space for deeper awareness of our true nature. This is where the magic happens and transformation takes place.

There is safety in being quiet, when others are reactive. Quiet defuses the situation, rather than adding fuel to the flame. Quiet brings understanding.

When our mind stills for a moment and we listen at a deeper level, it is truly an insightful moment to be cherished, no matter that it was just a moment. It's like an eternity, in spiritual time.

Nuggets of Wisdom II

A shift in our understanding can be so subtle that we may experience a quiet state more of the time and not realize this is our new normal. Because we've been used to more activity and stimulus from the outer world, we may not be entirely comfortable with the quiet. I know I wasn't. I felt a bit at loose ends when I wasn't always on the go. Consider exploring the new normal rather than reviewing old patterns of behavior which have previously filled our minds.

I'm seeing that living in peace and sharing love can help the world, without leaving my home. The spiritual energy we are made of ripples into the world of form, also made of spiritual energy, and calms the turmoil down in one way or another. Most times we may not be aware of this. It seems too simple. If we consider that at the very least, we're not adding to the stress in the world, we're adding love, that love has great merit.

Quiet the mind so the soul can be heard. Let your wisdom speak to you. Listen carefully. There may be some "doing" that comes to you in a common sense manner. When "doing" is driven by wisdom, Syd referred to that as *"doing without doing."*

23

Consciousness

Consciousness

Consciousness is more than "bringing our thinking to life." Consciousness is our awareness that we are form/formless.

Remember, the ability to notice is the Principle of Consciousness in action.

Mental health is not found through will-power. This natural resource already exists within us all. Mental health is simply realizing this spiritual fact and embracing it. That realization brings our spiritual power to life and changes the form of our world. Another way of saying this is, Consciousness is hope in action.

We can feel grateful for seeing what's "off" in our life as well as what's "right." It's a matter of how we see it. When we view our life with wisdom and understanding, it neutralizes judgment about right and wrong; from a neutral perspective, it's just information. This is where the principle of Consciousness plays its part in providing us with awareness without blame. How cool is that? Our lives improve naturally, from the inside-out, without us having to do anything, other than listen to our inner wisdom.

Too often we judge ourselves when we get gripped. Being aware when one is gripped is a good thing. It's Consciousness in action. Be grateful and that will release you.

I love seeing the fresh green leaves emerging in nature. Reminds me of us humans emerging into another level of consciousness; evolution from the inside – out.

Some think "Consciousness inside" is what is going on "inside of our heads" versus "inside" being inside wisdom.

Nuggets of Wisdom II

As my spirits and level of consciousness lifted, my observations of the physical world around me were enhanced.

***

Each person's response to a situation reflects their level of consciousness and their free will.

Seeing

To release true knowledge, one must learn to "see" versus "do." The "doing" happens naturally after the "seeing."

When I had a mild case of the coronavirus, March 2020, I experienced an exceedingly busy mind during the height of my fever. My personal thinking was going a million miles a minute. I felt like a hamster in a cage, going round and round. I hadn't experienced this busyness in decades.

What offered me a degree of solace was the fact that I "noticed" my busy mind. That was enough for me not to be totally gripped by my thinking. I didn't realize this until after my fever passed and clarity came to me. I simply experienced not being totally gripped.

While I was busy minded with fever, I could not abide television or reading. It was abhorrent to me. And I love both these things! Later, I realized that was Mind protecting me from outside stimulation to fill my mind even more. This was a powerful insight for me.

Nuggets of Wisdom II

In addition, I also noticed later that I wasn't judgmental about my busy mind. I didn't blame myself. I simply noted my experience. It was rather curious to me, as I hadn't experienced that busy minded feeling for a long time.

That noticing (Consciousness) gave me more understanding of the power of Mind, protecting me, during the fever. It brought me more compassion for others experiencing busy mindedness. As I rested in this new understanding, I could see how this applies to every single human being. We all are protected by Mind, Consciousness and Thought, hidden within our true nature; our spiritual inheritance.

Once again, learning the same message: "Seeing" is Consciousness in action, whether we are seeing good or not so good. When we see that, it lessens judgment of ourselves and of others. Now that my mind has cleared, I feel grateful for just "seeing."

It's not about doing; it's about "seeing" (Consciousness). Then the doing is spontaneous, driven by insight.

When we're unhappy that we're "seeing" old habits and wanting more insight on how to move past them, we're not seeing that we've already moved past them because we "see" them. Focus on "seeing" versus wanting.

To judge another is based on ego; to "see" another is based on wisdom.

When someone continues to act out after we've shown as much love and understanding as we can, let's not be discouraged. "Seeing" the psychological innocence in the person—they're doing the best they can, given their level of understanding-- neutralizes the situation. This allows us to take the high road and see what's right versus what's wrong. Then the answer we seek will come.

Thought

Thought

Consider the nature of Thought – not the form of our thinking. The nature of Thought is formless energy. It's our spiritual power to create our moment to moment experience. Our personal thinking is form; our personal thinking can take us down the path we want to go as well as the path we don't want to go.

～～

We are the thinker; we use thought to articulate our insights and bring them to life, thereby creating our moment to moment experience.

～～

The difference between examining our thoughts versus creating our experience is the difference between "what we think" versus "that we think." That we think lends itself to neutrality, seeing thought as a power; what we think leads to form and the creation of reality.

Elsie Spittle

In the early days, I didn't see that we all do the best we can given the state of our thinking in the moment. I saw life through the eyes of my thinking. Grateful now that I "see" life more of the time through the eyes of love and wisdom.

Underneath our personal thinking a nugget of wisdom may be hidden, prompting us to look at our life. The trick is not to judge ourselves or get gripped by our thoughts. Simply pause for a time and the treasure will reveal itself.

Refection stills personal thinking so that original thought can be heard, recognized, and put to use.

It feels so good to do something kind when we're feeling in a low mood; all of a sudden, the low mood is gone. . .our thinking has shifted so our mood has shifted.

Don't look for blame; look for resolution, from a calm state of mind.

Reader comment: "We've been reading your book, *"Nuggets of Wisdom."* It couldn't have come at a better time for us. We read a little, sometimes repeating it out loud to each other. And then step away from it. "Living in the present and remembering that my thoughts are a rudder." Wow. Really good and I really like the format. Thank you! I am going to read *"Our True Identity"* again."

I Know, But....

To deepen our understanding, it's important to set aside, for a moment, what we already know. If we keep what we know on our mind, there will be little room for new insights. There's an old saying about emptying the vessel before adding new wine. . . I find that very apropos.

We humans tend to honor the intellect and say "I know, but..", instead of honoring 'I know' and ignoring the 'but.' I "know" is wisdom; "but" is the intellect.

Honor "seeing" the dip in understanding rather than focusing on the "dip" of I should've, could've, would've, if only, etc. Don't waste time entertaining the "should've" in conversation with yourself or with clients. This leads to debate. Stick to the truth and purity of "seeing." This promotes soul to soul conversation.

Nuggets of Wisdom II

We're hardwired for happiness. We're born with original innate health, even if we don't know it.

Someone tells me he's "seeing" beyond culture, ethnicity, and so on. "But," he says, "I know there's so much more to see and I don't know what else to do to get there." Innocently, this soul has been rather dismissive of his "seeing power." He's focused on what isn't rather than what is. When we focus on "seeing" what is, for example, seeing beyond culture, ethnicity, and so on, that's a huge shift in consciousness, in knowing that we're all the same under our various disguises. This, this is "what is"!

Thought or Illusion

Joining Facebook has been an intriguing experience. My mind had been made up that Facebook would add more details and complexity to my life. I like a simple, uncluttered life and having "space" in my head for new thoughts to emerge. That's a nice place to live. . . however, the thoughts of maintaining my simple life closed me off to the advantages of Facebook, in regard to sharing more fully the gift of the Three Principles. When a dear friend pointed out the benefits of Facebook and educated me on how I could control the volume of "friends" and still share this message of hope and transformation, I found myself more open to joining. Bingo! I found myself in a new world, the wonderful world of social media. . . and saw, once again, the illusionary nature of reality. What I once thought, no longer looked the same. Illusion or reality?

Rather than ponder on how compelling thoughts and reality are, consider contemplating the illusionary nature of thought and reality. When our thoughts change, reality changes. Evidence of the illusionary nature and power of Thought. How can reality change if not illusion to begin with? How can reality change if it isn't formless energy, continually changing shape via our power to think? Freedom!

⸻

When we realize we're in our "head," caught up in personal thinking—sit back and relax as best we can. Let our wisdom guide us. We may think "I don't know what wisdom feels like but I know I've been in my head." That "knowing" is wisdom. We know we've been in our head. Now we're not. Knowing that feels good. Feeling good releases stress. Simple.

Feelings

Feelings

I've never experienced so deeply the meaning and results of the gift of deep feelings and our true nature as I did during a recent weekend gathering. I felt and observed: the mingling of spiritual souls merging as One. The richness and depth of feeling was so profound and filled with love, which provided a foundation for many to share their deepest understanding, emerging from each soul present. The cross pollination among the audience prompted insights popping in the moment.

I've never seen more clearly that the individual souls in the audience are taking the new learning they've experienced to help the world via "spiritual mentoring," simply by living more deeply in the feeling of their true nature. I feel blessed to be a part of this great mystical journey that Sydney Banks uncovered.

When we start to override the simplicity and feeling of the Principles with too much form, we lose the feeling and the impact. Let's not forgot that the Principles are the source of experience, manifested in the "feeling" of our true nature. That deep feeling is where all the answers reside.

Sometimes it's easy to slide into trying to "fix" people, despite knowing that each person has innate wisdom within. The quality of "feeling" of the interaction once again alerts us and helps us to stop, look, and listen. . . and slip into love, where understanding and solutions are born.

Communicate when the "tone" is right. Non-verbal judgment can be felt just as much as verbal. Once again, it's the feeling that is the guide and educator.

See beyond "living in the feeling of our thinking." The focus tends to shift onto what we're thinking/feeling rather than the wonder that we have the gift and power of "Thought" to create. Once we see this, our life becomes easier, gentler, more harmonious. Then, as Syd so often advised us, *"just live."*

Nuggets of Wisdom II

The feeling of connection is the most important element in teaching/mentoring. The rich feeling of our core essence is what opens the door to the soul. Understanding and healing flows from that space.

⁓

When we stand strong in truth in the midst of others' confusion, the feeling of certainty supports us, even when we can't quite articulate our understanding. The feeling helps the message "land."

⁓

I remember in the early days, doing a day long session for a group of attorneys. I was feeling confused about whether there were three Principles or four! At that time, there was general confusion about this throughout the Principles community. And as I shared that with the group, they looked rather puzzled— understandably. What was eye opening to me in the moment is that even in my confusion, I felt "at home" and comfortable. The group picked up on my feeling of confidence and honesty, not my lack of articulation. As I continued my session, my certainty increased, and I "saw" that there are Three Principles, not four. . . .I was able to bring the group along with this fresh knowledge.

Later I shared this with Syd Banks. He got a good laugh from this. It also brought his attention to the confusion of the community and that it was time to do some in-depth mentoring with key practitioners to help them understand that there are only Three Principles and that everything else is created from these spiritual gifts.

⌒

Deep feeling is the groundwork for insight. The feeling is most relevant. When that feeling of wisdom is present, inner evolution is being done spiritually.

⌒

It's amazing how much learning this "stay at home" time is offering us during the coronavirus pandemic, spring of 2020. Yes, I know there is much suffering, yet there is opportunity. One thing I've learned is how rich a virtual retreat online can be. Pure energy meeting pure energy without the actual form of connection can bring even deeper connection. I had no idea the feeling could be so rich with depth and insight. A gift with unexpected rewards.

Insight

Honor Your Insights

Insight is a sacred space (spiritual intelligence) where the unknown becomes known. The more we honor that space, the more we are guided from the inside-out.

In the beginning of my inner journey, I always thought insight came with a big bang, given what I had observed with the profound insight Syd had. Then wisdom prodded me and I began to wonder if I'd been missing out by expecting too much. Many of the insights I've had, after my first realization that thought creates feeling, have been quiet and didn't seem like a big deal, yet the results of these so-called quiet insights transformed my life, and continue to do so. The quiet insights remind me of Syd's words: *"Be ordinary."* I wanted flash, not quiet. . . then I discovered the soothing comfort of quiet insights. Ordinary and extraordinary in one.

Insight resolved my dilemma. Insight brought about change. Then the path was illuminated with the light of understanding and patience. I found the best way to sustain change is to nurture and cherish the feeling of gratitude for every positive change that occurs, small or large—seeing what is right, rather than what is wrong in our lives.

Because insight lasts only a moment, some think it's a momentary understanding. They don't realize that insight brings about lasting change.

On my morning walk, mist covered the landscape. As the sun peeked through here and there, I could clearly distinguish the meadow and the trees. It struck me that occasionally insight is like that; it emerges in mist, then clears up and reveals deeper understanding. This is lovely, offering a mystical feeling of the illusionary nature of life.

It's fascinating to see how experience changes from one moment to the next. For example, let's say someone has a reactive experience and is thoroughly engaged in their personal thinking about the situation. Then they realize that "I'm okay if I don't think about it." Isn't it incredible that simple insight can totally change one's perspective and life?

Nuggets of Wisdom II

I love the simplicity of the Principles understanding. Once again, nothing to do but live in wisdom, our natural birthright, as best we can, and we'll be taken care of—from the profundity of insights to the practical transformation in our lives.

~~~~~~~

This is an insight shared by Paul:

"Just wanted to share that I was reading *"Beyond Imagination"* the other day and the beautiful feeling suffused in your words sparked in me the kind of feeling that I have only previously experienced when reading Sydney Banks's books.

"It also led to a wonderful insight about the power of the feeling. For some time, I have struggled to figure out how to integrate this understanding into my work. I'm a team leader, and so want my team to benefit from these Principles.

"What occurred to me while reading your words was that I've been trying to articulate the Principles, rather than communicate them through living them, through the feeling that living close to our true spiritual nature brings.

"It seems to me that if I show up to work and go through my day with appreciation and love for my co-workers, that will have its effect.

Elsie Spittle

"And if it doesn't, that's not my problem. Everyone has innate health, and I think I've spent too much time working on perceived problems, and not enough time appreciating everyone's perfection.

"Words are a poor substitute for my feelings of gratitude for the insight your works inspired, but many, many thanks."

Own your insights—it's one thing to respect the catalyst or person who helped spark the insight—it's another to honor your own wisdom. This neutralizes dependence on anyone or anything and opens the door to more insights.

As I'm enjoying the hummingbirds in our back yard, half hidden insights emerge, bathed in the light of understanding. Without words, the feeling of understanding offers tranquility, of being nestled at "home."

Wisdom

The Value of Wisdom

When intellectual thought is quiet for a moment, wisdom shines through and reveals our true inner identity. The intellect asks "why"—wisdom knows "why." I find that spiritual fact very reassuring.

We are born to share our wisdom naturally, with love; often non-verbally. It's the feeling of love and acceptance that brings about the connection between all life forms. When we're coming from love, we're sharing from "home" rather than teaching the Principles. The Principles are our home. This is the simplicity and profundity of our spiritual inheritance—home.

When we have a negative feeling, our wisdom hasn't left us. That feeling is still our wisdom, our guidance system, a gift from our true nature. It tells us we're off track. We don't need to figure out why we're having that feeling. "Seeing" the low feeling automatically moves us back into well-being.

Elsie Spittle

When indecision comes upon us, the best thing to do is— nothing. Be patient and let wisdom rise to the surface to guide. Sometimes this is very difficult as our personal thinking continues to be circular, keeping us in a busy mind. Still, I'd rather wait it out and let wisdom guide. Wisdom is always along for the ride.

Isn't it amazing that when we don't intellectually analyse our problems, we find the solution "inside" our wisdom. Less analysis equals more clarity. I love this!

Ask wisdom for answers and wisdom responds. This is evidence that the Principles are: a) dependable b) universal c) always available, whether we know it or not.

It feels so good to thank our own wisdom, when it grasps our hand and pulls us from an old habit that we've slipped into. It may be "over thinking, over eating, over drinking, over judging." Whatever it is that continues to provide an opportunity to learn and grow. Wisdom dissolves guilt. How awesome is that!

Nuggets of Wisdom II

Trust your own wisdom; leave space in your mind for original thought. Stop the search and discover the treasure within.

Sometimes when we feel wisdom is driving us "beyond our limits," is it really wisdom energy or is it ego energy that is in operation? Both are the same energy, used in different ways. We can feel the difference if we slow down enough to allow our divine wisdom to guide us.

Ego protects the personal self; wisdom promotes Universal Self, which enhances the personal self without having to prove ourselves.

Pure truth lasts the test of time. Copying someone else's truth fades with time. Truth stirs the soul and brings light to our world.

Elsie Spittle

It's a blessing to trust in the patience of spirit. Patience from spirit brings clarity and hard decisions become clear.

~

"Responsibility" from wisdom is light as a feather. "Responsibility" from the intellect can be heavy and weigh you down. It's our choice.

~

What a blessing it is that the 3 Principle community is sharing around the world at this time, when the world is going through so much physical and mental suffering. People are offering love, wisdom and stability. I remember the month after 9/11, Syd was about to do a conference in Hawaii. We all thought he should cancel it because people were so nervous of travel and were frightened of more tragedy. Syd was adamant that he continue with this seminar. He said this was the time when people needed the most help. Ultimately, it was the best conference he ever gave. Participants responded to his unconditional love and lack of fear, and gained strength by seeing his example. Live in wisdom and trust that all will come right.

Nuggets of Wisdom II

Wisdom could care less about the form and yet it is through wisdom revealing itself that the form is enhanced.

When behavior changes, we tend to compliment the change in behavior and that's great. Everyone enjoys being noticed for the positive transformation. Something to consider is that it's equally helpful, if not more helpful, to acknowledge wisdom, where transformation comes from.

When we are functioning in our wisdom, we don't need to practice listening skills; we naturally listen better because our mind is clear. The simplicity of the gift of wisdom. Everything becomes more enhanced as we embrace our spiritual birthright.

When we're caught in the swamp of our thinking, look to the feeling we're in, full stop. The feeling tells us we're off track. That's all we need to know. When we do our best not to entertain "why" we're in the swamp, this will allow wisdom to once again rise to the surface and light the way to clarity.

Elsie Spittle

When I began to dip my toe into the water of true knowledge, I gained strength, confidence, and a willingness to be scared and still move forward.

How refreshing for our clients when we meet with them and don't have expectations—because we "know" if they hear their wisdom, they'll live up to their potential and more. "Knowing" eliminates expectations and provides a clear path for us and our clients.

Wisdom or distraction? Sometimes Syd's teachings are being used in a way that, innocently, distracts people from their own wisdom. We all interpret Syd's words through our own level of consciousness, and that's where the purity of the message can get lost. Then we share our innocent misunderstanding and often times confuse people. They may not trust their own wisdom, even though their wisdom is prompting a question deep inside. Is what this teacher says true or is what the other teacher says true?

This is why it's so important to point people to Syd's original message of simplicity versus complexity, of stillness versus noise, of love versus ego. The purity of Syd's message will awaken the soul to trust their own wisdom more.

Free Will

There is a huge difference between free will and will power. Free will is freedom of choice. Choice is based on "understanding" the role and power of the Principles; understanding that we have the gift of being able to create our experience. Honoring the gift of "creating" brings peace of mind and eliminates the feeling of "control."

Will power comes from the intellect; it is not based in understanding. Will power is based on personal control - "I WILL do this." Control comes from the intellect feeling like we NEED to do this in order to succeed. It's about ego power.

Free will provides us with choice—do we want to live in the feeling of love and well-being or not? We have the support of wisdom. To not use it is a disservice to Self/Mind.

Elsie Spittle

Why do humans get so busy minded if we're hard wired with innate mental health? Free will is our gift from understanding the Three Principles and how we use them for creating experience. It's the game of life. We get to choose how to use the Principles, in a healthy, productive manner or in a less healthy manner.

⁓

When we're gripped by the intellect, our free will really comes into play. We have the choice to use pure energy of Mind in a personal way or to allow wisdom to emerge. Knowing this brings a very deep response and cleans up our life.

⁓

Although we can't "control" our thoughts, we can choose a direction we want our thoughts to flow. Here's where free will or choice comes in. Instead of focusing our thoughts on what's "wrong," focus on "what's right." The feeling of judgment will dissipate; clarity and wisdom will emerge, offering a solution. When we're in the feeling of judgment, there is no clarity. When we're coming from wisdom, solutions appear, seemingly out of the blue.

Our True Nature

I'm once again humbled by the power of this inner spiritual essence, providing us with true knowledge. I continue to learn that insights are a gift from our true nature, Mind. I love the simplicity of this learning. Offer your heart and soul via a feeling and people wake up. . . oh my. So wonderful to see/feel so many more souls awaken to the simplicity and power of our true nature emerging. It's so beyond us and yet comes through us. A mystical/mysterious journey.

⌒

The power of sharing truth with simplicity is that it draws out that deep feeling, the essence of our true identity. Here is where all our questions are answered. The more we point people to their true identity, who and what they really are, spiritual essence, the more their souls are awakened.

⌒

When you've experienced the deep feeling of our inner essence, know this is available always. See this beyond possibility to "spiritual fact." This is honoring our innate inheritance.

Elsie Spittle

Isn't it a great feeling when you're spring cleaning your home or closet of unwanted items? Sometimes it takes a bit to let go of those familiar objects. . . but the reward is less clutter, more space to find things. It's a little like spring cleaning one's mind, when unwelcome thoughts persist. In a burst of insight, one's mind is cleansed of clutter and more space is available for our true nature to expand.

When a quiet moment naturally occurs in conversation or a presentation, cherish it; let it ride. It's our true nature connecting with others, without words.

Discovering who we are on the "inside" leads to a life where even in challenging circumstances, we have a constant "friend" who will support and uplift us, who we can count on without fail. That "friend" is our natural, innate wisdom—our true Self.

Last public talk this evening, in London. Fabulous gathering! I'm so moved by the responsiveness of the audience. Each person has embraced the 3 Principles understanding with open arms. To know that each soul that has been touched then goes into the world, and simply by being more fully awake to their true nature, awakens others, is beyond description. I'm in awe.

Love, compassion, deep listening and neutrality are inherent to our true nature. Deep listening in and of itself has the power to heal mental stress.

It's the feeling of our own true nature that opens the door to a soul-to-soul conversation with other people. It's in the richness of a deep feeling that our true nature is touched. It's the "feeling" that is the educator. We are, indeed, a vessel for the spiritual essence.

The more we release our true nature, the more we become "whole." No dependence on another is needed when we are in alignment with our inner spiritual core. The wholeness or Oneness we experience in alignment gives us the confidence to stand alone, knowing we are complete. Then, when we join with others, it is with great joy and harmony.

Elsie Spittle

A story that may appear frivolous or seem to lack relevance, but is told with deep feeling, can turn out to be a most meaningful nudge in the direction of our spiritual birthplace, our very essence within. I shared a story at a retreat about buying new shoes, and described the joy I experienced while trying on the shoes. My enthusiasm brought a good deal of laughter to the clerks who were assisting me. One clerk who was about to leave for the day, actually took off her coat and set it down, and stayed to join our fun.

I didn't think anything profound would occur at the retreat because of that story; I just shared because it came to me in the moment. I could "see" the audience relax as I shared this lighthearted event, and in their relaxed state they were more attentive as I carried on.

Some time later, I got a beautiful letter from a woman who had attended the retreat, who was deeply struck by the "feeling" of my story. She told me that she felt uplifted for several weeks after this and wondered how it was possible to be uplifted from her depression to the point of gaining insight, while the story I shared was so simple and seemingly unimportant.

She told me that her life had changed, had become easier, and that she's trusting her wisdom more. Her story really touched me—a beautiful transformation—all because of a feeling that arose from a fable about new shoes.

Nuggets of Wisdom II

When we "stand in wisdom," a feeling of gentle certainty is born that helps point people inward to their divine nature, simply by the feeling coming through us. The feeling draws out their true nature, and they become their own teacher. Such is the magic of our inner spirit.

Understanding

What's been striking me recently is how powerful inner honesty is in assisting us to evolve into our true nature. Inner honesty doesn't come from the ego or intellect. It comes from "home," the essence of Mind that resides within each and every one. Mind gently nudges us to look deeply at where we want to live; in judgment and blame, or in understanding with compassion. When the prodding feels hard or difficult, that speaks to our ego getting in the way. When the nudge is gentle, that is wisdom whispering in our ear.

Listening with a quiet mind provides us with an open channel to hear wisdom, ours and the individual or group we're listening to. Listening in this way provides a flavor of health, whereas listening to try and understand where they're coming from psychologically can sometimes move into analyzing content of thought. Deep listening allows us to float in the space of neutrality, and helps those we're listening to access their wisdom as well. Just as we are supported by water when we float, so does wisdom support us and provide buoyancy which propels us forward in true understanding.

Nuggets of Wisdom II

It doesn't matter how new or familiar one is to this understanding; truth emerges and collapses outer appearances. We truly are One spiritual essence.

~

To greet and honor life with gratitude, grace, and kindness in our hearts brings bounty to our life. The bounty of being freshly inspired to keep time for our Self and our family enriches our lives, allowing us to serve with more love and understanding. A win-win situation all around.

~

It may be hard to believe that when we assign blame to someone, we give away our spiritual power, leaving us with less understanding. Assigning blame comes from our ego, which covers up our clarity of mind and our compassion.

~

Accepting people where they are, with all our issues and so on, brings new understanding of who and what we are, spiritual beings housed in the physical form of humanity. That doesn't mean to say we have to stay in a toxic situation. I'm pointing to acceptance, in the form of neutrality and non judgment, understanding that we all do the best we can, given our level of consciousness in the moment. From this non judgmental space, mental healing can take place.

⁓

We don't have to understand people's thinking; that process only gets us mired in the "content" of thought. Rather, we simply want to see that people "think." This allows us to be compassionate and brings understanding because our own mind is not filled with personal thoughts.

⁓

Being on a plateau is a good thing—it lets you see with perspective. Then once you've seen all there is from that plateau, another comes along. This is called "infinity"!

⁓

My nephew is a priest, and occasionally he and I have had very deep conversations about God. We respect that we each see God differently and express our understanding differently; we're in alignment that there is a creative force behind life that powers humanity. I love the connection beyond the words that bring understanding.

Richness of Being

In continuing our inner evolution, living in our "being" as best we can is primary— "doing" is secondary. "Being" is spiritual— "doing" is physical.

⁓

So easy to slip into "doing" rather than "being." While we're focused on trying to stay in a good mood, or to shift others in that direction, we have moved into doing rather than being.

⁓

Something to consider. There's a weight to labels. We say "I'm depressed"; "I'm a cancer survivor"; "I'm a failure"; "I'm insecure," etc. And then we buy into our story and operate from the belief system of "what's wrong." We forget that we're more than our story, even in regard to surviving cancer. If we keep looking to surviving, we're not really thriving. We're living in the form of what's wrong rather than living in what's right.

When we're living in the moment, we're living in the moment of creation.

⁓

I'm taking it easy! Learning how to do "nothing" and enjoying it very much. In the quiet space of my mind, I can feel the creative juices perking. Doing nothing can sometimes be the most effective form of action.

⁓

I remember when I didn't like being on my own; I always needed to be with someone. Now I cherish time with myself uncovering the richness of "being." Then when I'm with others, I appreciate their presence even more. Who knew? The education continues.

⁓

Absolute joy to spend time with a dear client. Soul to soul connection and insightful conversations. Great fun exploring the island: sampling delicious goat cheese, admiring the wee lambs, and then doing some clothes shopping. The simple pleasure of "being" that opens the inner sanctum of wisdom and clarity.

Nuggets of Wisdom II

What a blessing to know that comfort and solace lies "inside," where our quiet strength is strongest. This is where our protection from the craziness of the world resides.

There are times when one may crave solitude, a different solitude from what we've experienced before, to find a new and profound peace nestled in the essence within.

The stillness of being in the moment: you can "hear" the sound of silence. It sounds and feels like a gentle "humming" of energy. The sound and feel is substantive. It's a sacred moment to be cherished.

Nourish the Soul

Nourish the Soul

It's so important to take time to cherish our spirit! Sometimes we may forget this and become overwhelmed with the amount of work we have to do. I know I do. Then I had an insight that stress is wisdom's way of telling us to slow down and take time for ourselves.

I'm listening to and cherishing the source of wisdom more than I did before. Being in service to the world is a blessing and a passion; however, all too often we forget our Self in our dedication. I'm learning to pace my time, to honor the value of slowing down. As a result, my life with Ken and with my Self is richer, simpler, and more harmonious. This translates into deeper sharing and impact with my clients.

Mother Nature offers beauty to nourish the soul. There is also great solace in nature! There's a wee garden outside my husband's home office window. We planted it in honor of his Mom who passed several years ago. The vines of wisteria and clematis are variations of her favorite color, mauve. I often pause by the garden and let the beauty fill my senses, as well as my memories of Mom. She loved the island, loved gardening, and loved Syd. He invited her to tea at his home when Mom visited us after Dad had passed many years ago, and Mom was filled with sorrow. When she returned from tea with Syd, she never told us what he said to her; however, her face reflected calm and peace of mind. I cherish this story.

~~~

There is such solace in this spiritual energy that we're made from, especially in times of need. We receive the gift of grace as a mantle of protection from challenging times. So grateful for this!

~~~

When we honor our soul, the deepest part of us, our soul will honor us. When we shed the addiction to our personal thinking, the world opens up to us, and love fills our whole being. LOVE is our being.

~~~

When I point my clients to Self-care, they think that's taking care of the body. Relax with a cuppa, eat healthy, time for a bath (with phone and tablet). Not much quiet there! The phrase "soul-care" came to me. "Space" for soul wisdom to emerge from vessel of our body. That's the gold!

Just when I think I've said it all, about my 44 years sharing the Principles, more feeling/words come out. I was asked to speak at a staff/volunteers gathering, at the end of several other speaking engagements. It still astonishes me that when there is such deep interest, it can draw more out of you than you thought you had to give. I felt spent, yet the responsiveness of the group touched my soul, uplifted me, and more energy poured out. However, now I'm "cooked"! Resting in my hotel before a very early flight to Spain to speak at the VIVA conference.

Soul to Soul

Our sole purpose on earth, as I see it, is to evolve as spiritual and physical beings. From this space, soul to soul connection has the greatest impact and is truly serving humanity. We use conversation to understand, not to convince.

—⁓—

To keep our relationships fresh and vital, it's so helpful to "see" each other as soul to soul rather than personality to personality. Focusing on personality can bring judgment or blame or wishing someone was different or . . . When we see beyond personality to someone's soul, this seeing brings understanding and love.

—⁓—

Occasionally I have clients who have deep held beliefs that suffering helps them to feel compassion. As I listen deeply to their story, I often hear a gem of wisdom, hidden in their belief system. When I ask them if suffering serves them well, and if they feel peace of mind, they pause for a moment. Then they say, "I feel no relief but. . . ." The gold is the "pause" and the honesty when they say "no relief." That is where I point them—the pause—the pause is wisdom giving them space to "breathe." I don't focus on why they're suffering. I focus on the pause and their honesty, which comes from their true nature, their wisdom. Now, we have soul to soul conversation.

I'm so moved by the response of the people at the Norway retreat, May 2017, hosted for me by Tore and Kari Skåtun, founders of the Norwegian 3 Principles School. I knew very few people, and it didn't matter, because once again, we had soul to soul connection. The power of this connection is beyond words and beyond description. I can only say, it was magical, and I'm humbled by that spiritual essence. My utmost gratitude to you all!

The release of wisdom contains a magical ingredient that facilitates a response from others of deep-felt joy and contentment. This is the soul to soul connection that all humans are looking for, whether we know it or not.

Elsie Spittle

The gift of "listening" is a magical gift for all seasons. It doesn't cost anything, yet the value is immeasurable. In the holiday season, it's easy to get overwhelmed and distracted by all the activities of shopping, planning holiday festivities, attending office parties, and so on. Taking time to really be attentive, to "hear" one another takes one to that inner place of calm and peaceful comfort.

Learn to speak to the inner core, where we are all the same, and where rapport and connection are made. When I realized this, all my relationships automatically changed for the better, without "having" to change them.

The gift of connection at a deep level with our true nature, with the essence of who we really are, offers a timeless moment to hear the whisper of soul. Refreshed, we can rejoin the world and celebrate our spiritual inheritance.

On my drive to the local farm to pick up vegetables, I often love to listen to Syd's tapes; and sometimes I love to listen to "nothing." "Nothing" is a rich feeling of contentment, wanting nothing. Wanting nothing is resting in soul space.

When we find our "wholeness" within us, this offers more love/impact to others. Wholeness=Oneness=connection.

I'm filled with gratitude for the soul to soul conversations we enjoyed in our Costa Rican retreat, October, 2019. The group was so receptive and shared with honesty, wisdom, and humility. The feeling of love and learning was expressed with many "apapacho" (hugs and cuddles). I loved it! I know we all are taking that feeling home with us, and it will ripple out and touch all those we come in contact with, planting seeds of true knowledge, a message of hope and transformation for Latin America countries.

Staying Grounded

Staying Grounded

The simplest way to deepen our grounding in the Principles is to honor our current grounding. This, in and of itself, takes us deeper into our wisdom.

~~~

In the early days of my sharing, I thought my grounding wasn't good because I compared it to my ability to articulate my understanding. When I got stuck in sharing my understanding, I doubted myself and doubted that I knew very much about the Principles. I asked Syd about this. This was his response: *"Share what you know and be quiet when you don't know what to say. Don't try and talk like me or anyone else. Share your story of how you've changed—your first insight. Just be yourself and share a feeling."*

~~~

As time went on, I discovered the truth of Syd's statement. Sharing is about the quality of the feeling we're coming from rather than our ability to articulate the words. It's the feeling that will touch the true nature of the other person. When we share from the intellect, it has a different quality of feeling, and chances are we won't have the same quality of engagement with another.

⁓

In response to a client comment: "My problem involves someone who is not listening to their wisdom, and no matter how much I'm listening to mine and trying to help them, they still don't change. . . what advice would you give?"

My response: "Have patience and trust their wisdom will come through, in their time, not necessarily in your time frame. I know this may sound easier said than done. However, staying grounded in our wisdom provides the patience and clarity of mind that will offer a solution. Wisdom also acts as a buffer, providing solace for us, and that's no small thing. When we are cushioned in solace, we come to understanding and compassion."

⁓

Even good memories and good intentions can get in the way of living in peace and harmony. We may live in our good memories, missing what's going on in our lives now. Intention is futurizing. "Living" is NOW. Sharing wisdom with others has more impact when we are living in the NOW.

Nuggets of Wisdom II

I had the perfect weekend—just lived in the moment, weeding the garden, enjoying the flowers. It felt like the best grounding for upcoming presentations; weeding my mind of extraneous thoughts in the silence of "now." Tending my garden—tending my soul; weeding my garden—weeding my mind.

Light at the End of the Tunnel

While in France on vacation, early Sunday morning, we strolled down the country road from our villa to explore the village, a medieval town called Séguret, in Provence. When we entered the enormous arched gateway into the community, it was as if we had stepped back in time. No residents were visible, no coffee shops were open, no tourists; we felt as if we were in an enchanted hamlet. As we continued wandering about, we spotted this narrow side street with the sun glowing at the end. We were captivated by the mystical charm and stood in silent admiration. The scene evoked an image of seeing the light of our true nature, shinning through the form of our physical being. The light that guides us home.

⌒⌒⌒

There are times when we feel lost; it's so helpful to know that when we persevere, we will find guidance once again from "home." Each time we go "outside" then come back "inside," we get stronger. It's a thin line, sometimes; yet that thin line is huge. A dear and wise friend put it this way: "It moves us from understanding to knowing." I love that!

Nuggets of Wisdom II

Just because we're living in mental health more of the time doesn't mean we won't occasionally experience bumps in the road. Mental health allows us to understand the bumps versus react, just as learning to drive around the bumps comes from understanding that we may hurt our vehicle if we go through them. Mental health allows us to avoid or maneuver around the bumps. Mental health is the light at the end of the tunnel.

Sometimes it's hard to listen to our wisdom because our personal thinking is so compelling. Nonetheless, even if we consider this, there are always moments of light that are available to guide us. Honor those moments and they will grow.

I want to share this message to me from a courageous soul. It touched my heart and brought home how profound the Principles understanding is; the healing power of the light of wisdom. "I've been battling anxiety and panic attacks for about 10 years. I'm starting to get some understanding from listening to you and Dr Bill talk about life. I'm seeing my life in a new way; it's hope where I was feeling hopeless. I'm still struggling with my condition but thru these teachings, I know I'm gonna overcome. It's like I keep getting glimpses of light. And my heart goes out to people who struggle like I do and someday I want to help others overcome. My struggles have been caught up mostly in feelings and emotions, it's been hard to get still and clear my mind. Thank you so much for sharing and doing what you do. God bless."

Be Gentle with Yourself

Embracing our humanness, with all the ups and downs, is a gentler way to see ourselves, rather than judging our human frailties. We all go up and down in levels of consciousness. This is perfectly natural. If we look at the "downs" as an opportunity to learn something new, it makes a world of difference. It simply looks like continuing education.

～

Don't judge yourself for moving past toxic relationships—that would be judging yourself for evolving with wisdom.

～

Our well-being is the most important factor in any relationship. When we take care of Self, we will be "residing in wisdom" where understanding and compassion come from. From this space, the gentle impact on others will offer solace rather than conflict.

Elsie Spittle

Cherish your spirit. Stress is wisdom's way of telling us to slow down so we can see beyond the form to the spirit.

Today I talked with those touched by cancer, who found hope in seeing beyond being survivors of cancer to finding their spiritual being. Others who experienced suicide situations also found a calming perspective. All were touched and there were tears of hope and relief. Terminal cases found hope in gaining understanding that we "go home" when we pass from this world of form; "going home" offered a fresh perspective and a deep source of comfort. I felt privileged and was very moved to talk with this attentive group, primarily Spanish speaking. Although my talk was translated for me with depth, the feeling needed no translation.

Spiritual and Mental Evolution

Spiritual and Mental Evolution

Sydney Banks stated unequivocally, shortly after his Enlightenment experience, that the three spiritual gifts he uncovered have the power to change the fields of psychology and psychiatry and alleviate the suffering of humanity. It feels like the dawning of a new era, now that more psychiatrists and psychologists, trained in the Three Principles, are talking about the Principles being the "cure for mental illness."

A whole new paradigm has been born. A paradigm of understanding that we are born with innate mental health. This is a profound shift from the traditional way the mental health field has had, of looking at dysfunction and trying to fix what's wrong with an individual, rather than engaging what's right.

When we engage the innate mental health in people, solutions arise from within. These insights highlight answers to whatever problems are being held because of misunderstanding who and what we are, at our core.

Elsie Spittle

We all hit barriers in our learning—it's part of our evolutionary journey. I've found that it's so helpful not to get discouraged when we feel stuck. Just see it as evolution, an inner evolution. When we're grateful for what we've already found, that gratitude is like a magic wand. Wave it over our "thought barrier" and those thoughts will start to disappear.

Sometimes when we have a shift in our understanding, it feels like we're in an unknown space. This can be a bit unnerving. We may even start to reconsider some of the work we're doing, as our work in the moment doesn't have the same energy. That too can be unnerving. However, if we "see" that the unknown is a gift, space to realize something new, then the unknown becomes fertile ground, cultivated and fertilized by thought, planted with the seeds of reconsideration by Mind. This is mental and spiritual evolution.

It's been an absolute pleasure having an opportunity to "see and hear" the speakers at the 3PGC event, April 4th – 7th, 2019, with fresh eyes. We've known each other from the early days of Syd's teachings and seen each other grow, slip and fall, stand up again and learn—spiritual evolution. To share our journey and learn with the participants is a privilege.

Nuggets of Wisdom II

The combination of deep profound feelings and lighthearted joyous laughter at this gathering was all encompassing. When we embrace the Principles more fully, seeing that we're always "home" and resting in that space, this is where solutions to global issues are revealed. I'm feeling very, very grateful to be part of this amazing community of loving, wise souls around the world. Our future is NOW.

Living in spiritual integrity as best we can will overarch every aspect of our life. This spiritual/mental position promotes inner evolution.

When we see poor behavior in people, it's so helpful to remember that in all of humanity, there's a "diamond in the rough" via each person's inborn spiritual core. This doesn't mean we tolerate or accept the poor behavior; I simply mean that we don't get gripped by the behavior—rather we see the diamond in the rough. Seeing the diamond brings clarity and compassion.

Elsie Spittle

There's a difference between having respect for the spiritual reality of life and KNOWING that life is a spiritual reality.

〜⌒〜

What a wonderful education this inner evolution provides. Do nothing and learn! I love the freedom this offers; just live life and we'll benefit by the simple unfolding from the university of life within us all.

Being in Service

Two more webinars to do before my retreat event. I love these webinars and recent conversations with clients, as they help prepare me for sharing. Even though I've felt weary these past couple of days before I began the conversations with people, I always pick up energy during the exchange. I love how that spiritual essence boosts the body and soul and turns on the tap of wisdom.

~

Sharing wisdom with people is an amazing, mystical experience. Deep quiet at times, light with laughter at other times, and feeling the power of sharing stories. Such a privilege to experience the power of essence with simplicity, the deepest respect, and with honor. Sydney Banks, what an extraordinary gift you left us and all of humanity. Beyond words now, and beyond grateful.

~

See the distinction between "holding" people accountable versus "helping" people be accountable. Holding = assigning blame. Helping = being in service.

Elsie Spittle

Acceptance of individual differences brings understanding of separate realities. Holding someone to our standards brings misunderstanding and judgment.

⌒

Serving others in whatever capacity unfolds for us in our lives fulfills our spiritual purpose—to share the gift of wisdom. Sharing wisdom is the greatest gift we can give ourself and others. Sharing truth with others awakens their true nature and brings the light of understanding that enhances all our lives.

⌒

This is an insight shared by Clare:

"Something that came to me after our call was how I have perhaps not appreciated how impactful my sharing of this understanding could be or has been – like I have perhaps been waiting until I have permission to call myself a teacher of the principles – and something shifted in me on our call – I saw that when I just look for opportunities to share and be connected to others through this work – permission is not required – I fall back into the feeling of home – and from that place I know that I can serve people more deeply."

Nuggets of Wisdom II

Wisdom = Service: When opportunity comes our way and we're feeling uncertain, the feeling of service will override our uncertainty.

⁓

I love the feeling of being in service to inspiration. Inspiration drives my writing. When inspiration is the driver, the material seems to write itself.

⁓

It's one thing to learn the 3 Principles in a classroom setting; it's another to "live our learning." Sometimes this "living" is so natural, we don't even realize it. It's only when someone points it out that we comprehend we're helping others by simply living in wisdom. There's an innocence and joy that arises when we assist from this space.

⁓

I hardly have words to describe the depth and richness of the "feeling" and learning that unfolded at the retreat in Lake Como. Right from the beginning the group felt like family and that spiritual connection continued to bloom. Ken and I are filled with gratitude for the privilege of sharing. Our deepest thanks to our exceptional hosts.

Elsie Spittle

Our last night in Menaggio. We head for Milan tomorrow, then home. It's been a joyous experience having Ken with me at the retreat, since he seldom travels with me on business. I've never seen Ken more relaxed and in service to others. His gentle spirit and honest sharing touched many. We are exceedingly grateful to all the participants who opened their hearts and souls. Arrivederci!

Feeling happy to share and draw out wisdom from lovely souls who came to Salt Spring Island for mentoring with me. Grateful to have such a beautiful location for us all to relax together and learn. I'm filling to the brim with the insights that are being born in the moment, simply by honoring and listening to each others' wisdom. Looking forward to see what unfolds tomorrow.

Definitely feeling blissful after a delightfully profound time with my guests. Here are my client's comments: "Hard to leave this beautiful slice of heaven on earth. So grateful for the learning, awakening and unfolding that I got to experience this week. Beauty in every form took my breath away. Thank you, Elsie, for your Momma Yoda wisdom on the Three Principles. Excited to see what's to come!"

Nuggets of Wisdom II

It's fascinating to know that true knowledge can be shared in an infinite variety of ways. There are no rules regulating how we are moved by wisdom to share true knowledge. We can be settled in a lovely room, simply having a deep conversation. Or having lunch on the beach, admiring the ocean in all it's beauty. Or driving around the island, listening spellbound to Syd's words coming from an early recording. In the stillness of our soul, Truth arises and blesses our life.

———

As helpers, it seems to me that our job is to share true knowledge as compassionately and simply as possible. It's our clients' job to "hear" or not. The feeling of love coming from us as helpers will open the ears of our listeners.

The Next Generation

There seems to be some concern about what will happen as the "pioneers" of the Three Principles pass on. I don't think that's a problem. Wisdom never dies! When Syd passed on, although his loss was so hard to bear, after a time our own wisdom came to the surface even more. I know this will continue to happen as us "elders" leave this physical realm as well. The next generation, and the next, and the next, will continue to share their wisdom with the world. Universal Mind has its own way of preserving the legacy of wisdom.

An amazing weekend retreat with a new group. An inspired program that really brought out the spiritual essence inherent in humanity. The deep feeling that manifested amongst us was a profound reflection of that essence eliciting new insights from us all. It does my heart good to see the caliber of practitioners going out in the world. It was an honor to be part of this gathering and an absolute joy to learn together, to receive the sacred bounty of insight. The perfect blend of our spiritual and human nature. I love these people and love my so called "work."

I have a number of young practitioners that I mentor. In our soul to soul connection, I also feel like I am being mentored via our conversations. I appreciate their fresh eyes and wisdom that helps me "see" what I take for granted.

It touched my soul to see how this next Principles' generation are stepping up to the plate to share their understanding with the world. With this depth of understanding coming from the younger practitioners, there is no stopping Sydney Banks' message of hope and transformation.

Syd always encouraged us to see our youth as wise leaders of our future. Let's help the world see that instead of engaging and focusing on differences between race, culture, politics, religion, and so on, let the feeling of love carry us past the differences to common ground. Here is where understanding is born.

The most amazing 3P UK conference yet, May 2015. An honor to be part of that spiritual connection with 600 people. Especially touching was the panel of youngsters who shared their understanding. Concluding that panel was the youngest plenary speaker, age 16, who inspired and touched everyone. Once again, Syd's prediction that our youth would lead the way is coming true.

A friend's email:

Hi Elsie...just read your post about passing on the principles to the next generation...and thought I'd share with you that it's happening in our life...my mum and dad lived their lives in a way that was directly influenced by Syd and you and everyone else, and I try to live my life in the same way with gratitude and possibly wisdom. My son just moved to another state a few weeks ago, and is working full time and got his own place in the first week of being there. Very proud of him, but what really made an impact on me, was when I spoke to him recently, he told me how grateful he was for all the great things that have happened to him. This is a direct result of my mum. She preached gratitude at every chance, and I am very aware of focusing on that feeling, and now my 18-year-old son is doing the same. When he said that, I felt a tremendous sense of relief, and the next thought I had was how proud my mum would be of him. Love you.

Nuggets of Wisdom II

Overflowing with feeling of gratitude for seeing how Sydney Banks message is sweeping throughout the world. 750 people, with over 30 countries represented at the 3 Principles conference in London, May 2016. All united in love and harmony. I loved hearing all the presenters, especially the panel of teens, our future leaders. After a few days rest, I'm off on another adventure.

Back home again, and so grateful for the privilege of mentoring the next generation. It's been a pleasure and great fun to spend time with my young client. Exploring the island, dining on our famous fish and chips, and having in-depth conversation. To see the impact of conversations that were simple, profound, and enriching brings me joy, and to see the impact on my guest is deeply moving. And last but not least, to enjoy the simple pleasure of shopping for hats can't be overstated....truly living in well-being, not just talking about well-being.

Travelling to Spain for the VIVA 2017 conference. The gathering was full of love and inspiration; profound and practical. A privilege to be part of this amazing event. All the presenters I heard had their own unique voices; authentic, original and full of heart. Special kudos to the hosts. They put their heart and soul into this occasion, along with their team, sharing with the world Sydney Banks' precious message.

———

My last, and the best 3P UK conference ever! (June 2019) Love was in the air from the moment the event started. Everyone "felt the feeling" and in doing so, contributed to the richness and depth of the event. Soul to soul connection and conversations. Hearing the passionate commitment of the next generations and the results they're achieving in the schools, prisons, inner city communities, recovery centers, and so on, makes my heart sing. I'm dancing the dance of joy, mindful of my rather tired body. Nonetheless, I'm filled with elation, knowing that this is my last conference, and knowing the next generation are serving humanity with clarity and love.

———

After one of my talks at the 3P UK conference, a young man, smiling, said to me, "Your session is aromatic." I thought it was an odd and interesting statement. "I've never heard that before," I replied. "You have an original way of expressing yourself. I really like that." I repeated what he said. He burst out laughing. "No! I said your session has an air of magic!" A delightful case of separate realities that brought about cosmic humor. To this day, whenever this moment comes to mind, it brings a smile to my face.

~~~

The Norway retreat I had the pleasure of facilitating in June, 2019, after my last sessions at the 3P UK conference, had "an air of magic" about it (also known as aromatic). A beautiful space, filled with laughter, joy, deep insights, and the hospitality that the Norwegians excel at. I felt so at home amongst the attendees, many new young people who became immediate friends, kindred spirits.

Seeing their faces light up as they gained deep insight brought us all a profound feeling of hope, knowing that the message Syd gave the world continues to blossom in our youth. I feel like the luckiest woman to share in the joy of discovering our true nature and seeing how we're always Mentored by Mind. Thank you, Norsk 3P Forum, for hosting this wonderful event. And thank you to all the amazing participants!

Gratitude

Gratitude

I used to think it was appropriate to feel gratitude when I was feeling good—I didn't realize how important it is to find a feeling of appreciation for what we've learned, even when we're in a low mood. If we can find that appreciation "inside," that means we're centered again, and the low mood will evaporate.

To help clarify the value of gratitude: Gratitude is a deep feeling that connects us to our true Self where wisdom is stored. This deep feeling releases insights, which help us evolve and move forward on our inner journey.

The desire to learn more can be a deterrent. Desire can add pressure to "trying" to know more, or to self improve. Desiring change in one's behavior can actually get in the way of succeeding. Desire can be a barrier to the naturalness of change. Desire leads us to believe that we don't have wisdom within us which naturally promotes change.

Elsie Spittle

I'm excited to share this from Jana: "I would like to let you know that your two articles I translated were accepted to the Czech journal called Medium. They should be published one by one in January and February issues." This news from Jana means a great deal to me as my Father was born in Czechoslovakia. Knowing that my articles may be read by residents of my Father's homeland touches my heart.

———

I was thrilled to visit Prague with my family in May, 2018. It was a very special time for us all. I got to speak a bit of the language I learned at home with my parents and was thrilled when some of the local residents understood my very poor accent. Still, we had a lovely connection which brought a smile to my face that refused to leave. . .

Love

We are beacons of light in the world; just keep shining! Love IS the answer. Clearly, the world is crying out for solace. Our outpouring of love will help the general public live in more peace and harmony. Why? Because all humanity is love, at their core, whether they know it or not; whether they live in love, or not. The gift of love is that every moment, we have the opportunity for our true nature to be awakened by love, regardless of the circumstances surrounding us.

My heart is overflowing with love for humanity; witnessing the unprecedented gathering of women and all of humanity around the world uniting in love, refusing to be laid low by injustice and tyranny. *"Love is the answer; when you share, always talk your highest."* Sydney Banks. *"When they go low, we go high."* Michelle Obama.

Love is conditional when we are in lower state of mind. We expect people to behave in a certain way and judge them or are hurt by their behavior. Take the feeling of judgment or hurt as a signal that our thinking is off and be grateful for that knowledge. Then love is unconditional once again.

Pure love eases pain, both physical and mental. Love can change (surpass) the biochemistry of the brain. Pure love is pure spiritual energy and has infinite power.

There are times when one is moved to be direct with another in regard to assisting one to "see." When we come from love and understanding, love acts as an anesthesia, allowing the truth to reach deep inside, beyond the cloud of personal thinking. Just as a surgeon cuts out the disease so can we cut the misunderstanding to the truth within.

In London now on the last leg of my journey home tomorrow. I'm so eager to see Ken and to be in my wee cozy home. This trip, May 2015, starting with the Devon retreat, then the 3P UK conference, and ending with the Norway retreat, has been the most amazing spiritual journey. Down to earth, yet magical. Feeling full of beautiful feelings, yet my "vessel" seems empty. Sad to be leaving, yet so ready to go home. As Syd so often remarked, *"This is the best job in the world. Just show up and share love."* Thank you, everyone, that I had the pleasure of meeting, and those that I didn't get a chance to meet, it doesn't matter. We're family, all of us together as one.

———

A big learning for me: being in the moment and standing in integrity with love, coupled with diplomacy. I was given the choice, after facilitating a retreat, to spend the evening with a large group of people or with my retreat hosts of three. I felt a momentary "I should go with the big group." However, I was spent, having given my all during the retreat. So, I listened to my heart rather than my head and said, "I'd love to spend the evening with you three." The result was a beautiful evening, where we got to know each other in a way that wouldn't have happened, had I not spoken up. All too often, "duty" or "I should do this" gets in the way of free-flowing love.

———

Another example of standing in integrity with love. A colleague had asked for feedback on his brochure. A sentence in the flyer about Thought didn't ring true for me. I hesitated to say anything, as in the past, I'd slipped many times into being the "3 Principles police" and would point something out that I felt was not honoring Syd's teachings. During those times, I had felt as if I was protecting Syd's legacy. Nonetheless, my comments were not always received with understanding. . .

After a month, this sentence continued to niggle at me, and I finally was moved to talk to my friend as gently and diplomatically as possible, mentioning this sentence that I felt was in error to Syd's teachings. I asked him to help me understand, and said that I hoped he was not offended by my question.

To my surprise, my friend received my feedback with the utmost grace, and said that he realized my question was coming from love, and because of that, was not offended.

He quoted another passage from Syd containing the sentence that I had questioned. Once I had the context of the passage, I could "see" the truth of the sentence. When we spoke again, he told me that he had added Syd's passage to his brochure, clarifying his original statement. We had the most beautiful conversation ever, deepening our relationship and the love we have for one another. Blessed by standing in integrity with love.

For those who struggle seeing others suffer, when we understand we create our reality based on our thinking, then we feel compassion, and don't get caught up in the suffering. Our minds will be clear, "seeing" beyond the suffering to the soul inside that remains pure. Often times this is where words are best left unsaid as a means of communication or trying to get the other person to hear. Just live in "love" as best we can. Love clears the wax in the ear so the sufferer is far more likely to hear.

Sometimes we may be in a position to meet someone from our past with whom we've had a poor relationship. Don't presume that we'll have no perspective. Our feelings may be different when we meet again because we've grown in our understanding. We may find ourselves feeling compassion. Whatever the behavior has been, mean spirited or whatever, it's because they're hurting inside. We're growing beyond that. We're "love" inside, and so is that person. Meet that person with love and chances are, they'll respond in a healthier manner.

It's been invaluable for me to "see" that the more we live in the present, the more we live in the essence of love. Then distance from loved ones is no more than a thought. We're always connected in essence.

Elsie Spittle

How wonderful to end my summer hiatus by celebrating our 55th anniversary, August 2018. It's been an amazing journey through many different phases in our lives. We met when I was 16 and Ken 17. I thought he was cute and a gentleman, and he thought I was exotic! We fell in love and married young. Both rather stubborn in the early years but the common ground has been the nourishing power of love. The understanding we gained from learning about our true nature has brought tenderness and patience.

I'm so grateful to Ken for his quiet strength, constant love and support. We still get the giggles together and I find that very endearing. There's no one I'd rather be with. I never knew that love could continue to deepen so you feel as one, and yet have independence. We're beyond grateful and feel blessed.

Living Life

Being Ordinary

Lovely to have disconnected from technology this weekend and to "see" the rebirth of nature emerge in spring; the fresh green of tender leaves peeking out in the sun. In the meadows, the wee lambs nuzzling close to their mothers warmed my heart and brought a smile to my face. I felt my true nature respond and expand. Such is the power of rest and then reboot!

I'm being a homemaker again, baking almond bread, loving the fragrance filling the kitchen. And in the enjoyment of being at home, just living my life, I'm reflecting on my new book and feeling that heaven is at home! So grateful to Sydney Banks, who opened the door to learning by sharing the joy he experienced in being ordinary.

I can remember driving down the road to his home and seeing him cutting the lawn with an expression of pure contentment on his face. I never knew one could experience such a deep, rich feeling, simply by doing ordinary chores. Prior to my learning about this understanding, chores were chores, a duty, not a joy. What a gift to realize that joy opens the door to learning, not only from Syd, but most importantly, from ourselves.

───────

I recall how often Syd talked to us about being "ordinary." *"It is in our ordinariness that we will find we are 'special,'"* he stated. In this culture of self-promotion, the profundity of his words has even more value. It's easy to be taken in by our own hyperbole, by our image of self importance. The "feeling" of what is real — our true nature—will ultimately guide us, if we listen.

So What?

One of my favorite insights is "So what?" in regard to slipping into old patterns of thought. I used to have such judgment about myself when I had thoughts of "I should know better," "Why is this happening to me?", or "I blew it again." You know the drill. Now I feel freedom from judgment because "So what?" has brought me acceptance and understanding for old habits. Acceptance is in itself a shift from judgment to discernment, to freedom. Understanding brought me a feeling of gentleness for myself. That's when change happens effortlessly and old patterns slip away. Accepting and honoring the formless will take care of the form.

We are all the same in this evolution. We all have personal thinking, and can get upset about things. So what? This is the game of life; continuing education. Syd called life *"a contact sport."* He said this was an opportunity to learn more. So why get upset when our thinking is less clear and it's time for more learning? The ability to let go of our upset and come back to our true nature is the gift and blessing of this understanding.

Elsie Spittle

Instead of trying to analyze why we are in a bad mood, there is great freedom in feeling, "So what"! We can still choose to linger with negative thinking, if we want. That's part of our learning. So what if we linger in low energy. When we've had enough, we'll naturally bounce back. Knowing our low mood will pass lessens the intensity, bringing relief and comfort.

～～～

All too often we may judge ourselves for not "teaching the Principles" in what we think is an appropriate manner. I've been there. . . and it's a captivating thought. Then I had an "Aha!" moment. It occurred to me: So what? It's natural to want to do our best to serve our clients, or share with our family and friends. Then those sneaky judgmental thoughts come to mind that we aren't clear enough, funny enough, wise enough, to share the Principles articulately.

～～～

Let that thought of "Am I good enough?" go, let it slip away to nothing. When I realized that my insecure thoughts were hampering my wisdom, my insight of "So what" if I'm not as articulate as others, opened the door to more security and confidence within me, and best of all, a deeper feeling coming from my wisdom that touched those I was serving.

When is Enough, Enough?

Society tends to look at achievement as a measure of success. In our exploration of the Three Principles, we often continue that same tendency; to look for more—more understanding, more well-being, more peace—more, more, more. It's our human nature.

⁓

When is enough—enough? If one has a glimmer of an insight, is that enough? If one's life has changed a little, is that enough? Enough can be a feast! It depends on our perspective and on our level of appreciation for "enough."

⁓

Our human nature is always looking for "more" while our spiritual nature is advising us to be grateful for what we have. How do we resolve this dilemma? Once again, the answer is simple: be grateful for what we have rather than wishing for more.

Elsie Spittle

Truth disturbs, and illuminates the path to well-being. Intellect hangs on to control via "should" and "but." I.e. "I should be more grateful" or "But well-being doesn't last." Delete should and but from your vocabulary. Our true nature is always grateful! It's our intellect that wants more and more and more.

As a helper, when someone is gripped by their thinking to the point of feeling hopeless, if you can help them see they've gotten quieter, and they say "maybe," that's a great start. Too often we look for "I get this!' and expect too much. "Maybe" is good enough for a start on the inner journey. It's an open mind, where insights can blossom that lead us to the light of understanding.

When we wish for more insights, the insights we have been privileged to receive don't look like enough. The barrier to gaining more insight is desire for more. When we're grateful for what we have, the grateful feeling is where insight is born and released to guide us in our lives.

Nuggets of Wisdom II

It's so important to pay attention to those moments of quiet that spontaneously occur when we are sharing with our clients or family and friends. Rather than trying to teach more when our clients have found that quiet place inside, it's like magic when we let the stillness teach. Trusting the quiet place is more than enough. That quiet place is wisdom.

If you don't care for yourself, then who will; if you don't care for others, then what are you; if not now, then when? If we wait until our life is "perfect" before we share our wisdom, we will wait until hell freezes over. . . .I've found that when I share the moments when I have felt in a low mood, or gotten upset about something, those moments can be even more helpful to those I'm serving; often, more so than sharing the beneficial things all the time.

Life is a balance between living in the moments of beauty and understanding, and living in a reality that is unsettling. Once again, as Sydney Banks so often said, *"Life is a contact sport. Knowing that we have wisdom inside provides a strong foundation to weather the storm."*

Living Life

I have travelled on my own a great deal, sharing this understanding. I love to "live life" in between my speaking engagements. I love to explore the area, go for long walks, shop for groceries, whatever takes my fancy. I find this grounds me in life and many insights come to me during this time of living life. So simple, yet so profound.

—⁓—

I saw the most incredible rainbow while flying on the seaplane to Vancouver, to catch my flight to London. It was a little choppy to begin with, then the flight levelled out. A rainbow completely encircled the plane while we were flying; this continued for some distance. It was an amazing experience! I've never seen anything like this. I felt enclosed and protected by this circle of shimmering beauty. When we landed, I asked the pilot what this phenomenon was. He said the rainbow was in a circle because we were seeing it from the air. I felt like "Elsie in wonderland." It was magical.

Nuggets of Wisdom II

Last day in Edinburgh. I wandered the Grass Market area and fell even more in love with the beautiful, vibrant city. Stories that Syd had told me about when he grew up here came to life, as I walked toward the castle, and finally wandered past where he had lived in the Leigh district. My heart filled as I contemplated my good fortune in having met Syd, and for Ken and I to have witnessed the extraordinary transformation in him after his Enlightenment. At times, when I ponder this event, it feels like a fairy tale.

Much as I've loved my time here in Scotland, I'm now very ready to head for home, and my dear soul mate, Ken. I'm bringing with me a bottle of single malt Scotch for him, distilled in the Leigh district where Syd had lived. I know Ken will be so pleased to receive this special gift.

Ken and I are eagerly waiting for the Seahawks and Panthers game on the telly! I can't believe what ardent fans we've become since I had the thrill of seeing the Seahawks play live! George Pransky took me to Seattle, after I became interested in the game on television, seeing Marshawn Lynch run the field, graceful as a dancer, pivoting and dodging the opposing players.

Elsie Spittle

As all the spectators around me hollered at the top of their voices, Seahaaaawks, I felt a wee bit shy about joining them. At first, I uttered a faint cheer, then as the game became more exciting, I got captivated by the energy and soon was yelling as loud as those around me. My throat was sore at the end, but I loved every moment.

George gifted us with Seahawk jerseys so when the game is on the telly at home, Ken and I don our jerseys and eyes are glued to the screen. The late Roger Mills would have been thrilled, as he so often tried, without success, to introduce me to football! You never know what life has in store. Change can happen, even with simple things like enjoying a football game!

⟋‿⟍

I'm enjoying some quiet time in Calpe, Spain, 2017, after my presentations in London. There is a Moors and Christian Festival this weekend. From my terrace, I can hear cannons going off, and see flashes of light and billowing smoke, as a re-enactment takes place of Moors landing on the shore to conquer Spain in 1744. A joy to watch with the crowd. We all became as children to get the best view, including me. I'm so grateful to enjoy wherever I am, to feel at home and to be comfortable with my surroundings.

Nuggets of Wisdom II

The day before Ken and I were due to travel to Menaggio, from Milan, in September, 2018, we explored Basilica di Saint Agnese, outside of the city. Majestic arched ceiling, with rich red tapestry draped at the head of the altar, inviting you forward to bask in the sacred beauty. I always feel solace in the spiritual space, especially when no one else is there – but One.

Ken and I had the best day with our Menaggio retreat hosts touring Lake Como on their classic boat made by Riva. The best preparation for the retreat tomorrow; filling our senses with beauty.

After the retreat, Ken and I had a wonderful day exploring Bellagio on Lake Como. Loved it! Such a picturesque village, with its steep stone stairways and magnificent architecture. We missed having our family with us, yet it was wonderful for Ken and me to discover that as we explored the area, we were also seeing newness in each other. And to top it off, we had the best pizza ever!

Perfect end to another epic journey, travelling on my own this time, from a day spent with the One Thought Alumni gathering, to my last 3P UK conference, June, 2019, both these events in

Elsie Spittle

London. Finally ending my trip doing a retreat in Norway for Norsk 3P Forum.

The day after the retreat, during a walk through a path winding past a local lodge and campground, my hosts and I were invited to taste Norwegian waffles that were being cooked on an outdoor camp stove. The waffles were the best I'd ever tasted; thin and delicious, not thick like they are in North America, and served with sour cream and homemade strawberry jam. My mouth is still watering!

We thanked the cook and spoke to the group sitting around a picnic table. Of course, they noticed my accent and inquired where I was from. I told them I was from Canada, and one of the senior ladies said, "Do you know Ed? He's from Edmonton." I had to smile at her sweet question. I live in British Columbia, a completely different province. It was such a lovely connection, to spend some time with this group of seniors.

As we moved on our way, the cook told my hosts how much it meant to the group, for us to stop and talk with them, as they were from a live-in seniors' residence, and didn't get to meet many new people, especially from other countries. I was touched by this remark and thought to myself, how lovely to connect, heart to heart, wherever we find ourselves. Underneath our different ethnicities, we're all the same spirit.

Nuggets of Wisdom II

On our walk, we were heading to Land's End lighthouse. The restored lighthouse is from Viking times, I believe. The lighthouse keeper would light a fire in the wire mesh box to alert passing ships of dangerous rocks and so on, in the ocean. The whole place felt "out of this world" to me, so beautiful.

Now I'm ready for home, via Oslo, London, Vancouver, Salt Spring Island. I don't know if or when I'll be back in Europe again. I will say that sometimes I feel as if I've lived in a dream, travelling the world, sharing this transformative message that Syd gifted to the world.

Syd predicted that Ken and I would travel the world, if we HEARD him. I thought his prediction was a fairy tale. And in some ways, it has been a fairy tale. How did I get to be so lucky? Sometimes travelling with Ken, and much of the time on my own. Learning so much from each and every soul I came into contact with, and from each and every trip. Primarily, learning that home is where you are located. Home is "inside." Home offers confidence, safety, joy, and insight.

Living Life with Family

Ken and I had a wonderful weekend in Tofino, on the west coast of Vancouver Island; a delightful, relaxing time. The weather was perfect so we walked on the beach in the morning, and hiked the Rainforest Trail in the afternoon. Magical! So beautiful with the sun shining through the ancient trees, covered in moss, and then coming upon a lush fern garden. We loved it. The connection with nature nourished our souls.

I'm on vacation in beautiful lodgings in Bali, Indonesia. August 2015. I'm delighted to be travelling with our daughter Lynn, and daughter-in-law, Kim. I'd forgotten what it felt like to sink into the warmth of the sun's rays, letting the world drift by like the wispy clouds above. I was hesitant to journey this distance without Ken, yet it is turning out to be a blessing to have "girl time" with Lynn and Kim.

We're leaving our oasis in Candidasa and heading for the island of Lombok on the next leg of our adventure. I'm having such a wonderful time with my "girls." The staff at our lodgings have been so kind and hospitable to us, ensuring our every comfort.

When we've walked into the small village, we can see how poor the surrounding area is, yet the people seem happy and peaceful. This touches me, coming from a North American culture, where materials things are so important, and many count on this for their happiness. To find some degree of peace, within a poor environment, shows me that everyone has the ability to appreciate "what is" rather than "what isn't."

I've been working on my new book in Lombok, sitting by the pool overlooking the ocean. In the distance, I can hear the haunting evocative call to prayer from a Mosque. The sound touches my soul. A beautiful compliment to the deep feeling I have as I do a final polish to my book.

We're having our last dinner and last sunset in Lombok. I've loved my time in Indonesia and I know I will cherish this time forever! We met many warm-hearted people who hugged us when we left. We even met a mafia boss at a local cafe who was kind to us, and with whom we enjoyed interesting conversation. I became known as "Mama" at our lodgings and at the small café we frequented, and I was treated with loving respect. This was a moving experience for me, as I was a stranger in their land, yet we "felt" connected to each other. My heart is full.

We're now in Barcelona after long, long flights. After a day of rest, our energy restored, we started exploring, and fell in love with this magnificent city. Tree lined spacious streets, very clean. A startling difference after the poor infrastructure in Bali.

The architecture nearby is breathtaking. We stand in awe, taking photo after photo. Tomorrow we're going to Park Güell, designed by Gaudí. It's Lynn and Kim's anniversary, so this tour will be a wonderful way to celebrate their marriage. I know it will be a memorable day with two who are so dear to my heart.

A few days later, we toured Sagrada Família. The Sagrada Família is a one-of-a-kind temple, for its origins, foundation and purpose. Fruit of the work of genius architect Antoni Gaudí, the project was promoted by the people for the people. Five generations now have watched the Temple progress in Barcelona. Today, more than 135 years after the laying of the cornerstone, construction continues on the Basilica and is expected to be completed in 2026.

Nuggets of Wisdom II

It was the most awesome experience. The front of the Basilica looks like it grew out of the earth, organic material molded by Mother Nature. We were moved to tears upon entering, so strong was the feeling of spiritual essence. As we finished our tour, we were left humbled and contemplative. Truly an honor and privilege.

Our next stop in Spain was the charming town of Estepona. We ended up staying near here by accident. Had totally planned to stay elsewhere; however, our accommodations did not turn out well. The beds were unmade, there was dirty laundry in the washer, waiting to be cleaned, the floors were dirty, and so on. We were a bit perturbed, then just let it go.

The next morning, the three of us went for breakfast and while we ate, discussed our next step. We went with the flow and the girls viewed other lodgings on their phones. Kim found something much better for us. It also felt like Mind had something to do with keeping us calm and helping us trust that we'd be okay. It felt like Mind was guiding us. . . So grateful for the practical and profound.

Elsie Spittle

I celebrated my 70th birthday with Lynn and Kim in enchanting Estepona. They treated me to a gourmet dinner, and gifted me with an exquisite Spanish handbag. Ken's gift of pearls from Bali warmed my heart and my ears. . . I felt like a kid, getting spoiled by my family. Before I had left for my trip with the girls, my son, Ron, and his wife, Lori, had sent me a card and gift. Although we were separated by distance, I felt all my family were with me in body and spirit.

The next day we explored the cliffside medieval town of Ronda, settled in 600 BC by the Celts. An unbelievable twisting drive through the mountains to get to the town. Once there, we were struck silent by the magnificent scenery!

Much as I have loved my time exploring Bali, Lombok, Barcelona, and Estepona, I'm ready to head for home. Tomorrow I start my journey to London, then home to my dear man, Ken. Lynn and Kim will continue their travels to Portugal, and explore that area.

My adventure with the girls is something I will treasure forever. We spent 7 weeks together, sharing lodgings, cooking together, and at times, doubled over with laughter; then having quiet time apart from one another, giving each other space to just "be." The perfect travel companions.

Nuggets of Wisdom II

Ken and I are on another family trip with Lynn and Kim, May – June, 2018. We landed in Paris, and after a good night's rest we're off to see the magnificent Sacré-Cœur and explore this stunning Basilica. We caught a glimpse of the Eiffel Tower from a viewpoint at Sacré-Cœur. I never, ever imagined I'd be privileged to see exquisite Paris. I'm pinching myself. And to top it off, I found a gorgeous pair of red shoes. I hesitated to buy them but I'm going back later to purchase. They're just right for Mama.

The family has gone to another Market. Mama is having a "rest" day, after having explored a wonderful Market yesterday. I've never seen such a magnificent array of produce. We brought some home to sample. Superb flavor of heirloom tomatoes, avocado, mangoes. Oh my! I'll stop now.

What a crazy morning at the Musée du Louvre! We were so excited to go; however, we didn't anticipate the masses of people. It was Labour Day holiday. Even though we bought advanced tickets and arrived early, it was super busy. We couldn't get through the crowd to get a close up look at the Mona Lisa, so we had to be content to view this famous artwork from a distance. I was so happy that Ken, with his height, was able to zoom in with his camera and take a great photo, so that I was better able to view the famous smile of Mona Lisa. We had better luck with touring Napoleon's apartment. It was amazingly ostentatious. After that, we were glad to get back to our apartment, put our feet up, and have an Irish coffee.

We've had a wonderful week in Paris. We explored many side streets, with cobblestone sidewalks, and cafés tucked in a corner. We sat at outdoor tables, drinking our expresso, watching Parisians and tourists stroll by, with their baguettes sticking out of shopping bags. We toured the Seine River on a river boat, admiring all the scenery; the Eiffel Tower, Louvre Museum, and many more historic sites. On our return boat journey, we disembarked near the Eiffel Tower and enjoyed a glass of wine at another café, drinking in the ambiance of the majestic Tower, as well as the tasty wine. We loved this beautiful city. Such a wonderful time with family, exploring the magic of the city and enjoying every moment.

Now we are heading for Normandy. We rented a car from a car hire place, near our apartment in Paris, and Lynn drove through Paris all the way to our next destination in Normandy, La Goulafrière.

Nuggets of Wisdom II

Ken and I and Kim were so grateful to Lynn, for her courage and skill at navigating through Paris during rush hour. Ken and I sat in the back seat; I had my arm tucked within Ken's arm, and occasionally I gasped, as we came to a close call with another vehicle. Lynn and Kim were pretty nonchalant about the whole thing. They are very seasoned travellers, after having travelled throughout parts of Asia for a year and a half. Once we got on the motorway outside Paris, I relaxed and enjoyed the ride. It felt like Ken and I were the kids in the back seat, while our parents, Lynn and Kim, drove us to our next lodgings. Definitely role reversal happening and we're loving it!

~

We're having a wonderful rest in the sunshine of Normandy. Our rustic lodgings are surrounded by nature and fragrant fields of golden canola. From here, on a day trip, we visited Étretat, with its amazing cliffs and rock formations. We stretched out on the meadow of grass, overlooking the cliffs, and savored life.

~

On the way to our next lodging further north, Glatigny, we stopped at Beuvron-en-Auge, one of the 10th most picturesque villages in Normandy. We were enthralled by the beauty. And the homemade apple cider was lovely too!

Elsie Spittle

While we were staying in the gorgeous home we'd rented, near Glatigny, we found an old tandem bike tucked away in a corner of the garage. "Old" is the operative word here. . . The adventures of Elsie and Ken on the tandem bike says it all! I was on the back wobbly seat, Ken in front, wearing a biking hat with the brim backwards. With his slim frame and the hat brim backwards, he could have been part of the Tour de France bike race. Kim steadied Mama till I got a bit of balance, then gave us a wee push, while Ken peddled like mad. I was hanging on for dear life. My feet didn't reach the peddles, so for some reason, I ended up sticking my legs out sideways; perhaps to gain some much-needed balance. At this point, we all were laughing so hard, I could hardly catch my breath. What a joyful experience. Learning to be kids again, supported by our kids.

After a few days, nestled at our lodgings, enjoying doing nothing, relaxing on the cushioned lounge chairs, cooking on the BBQ, we feel ready for more exploration of our region. We're heading for Mount Saint Michel, a UNESCO World Heritage site, about an hour and a half from Glatigny. After parking the car, and beginning our walk across the causeway, we had to stop, and drink in the magnificence of the Abbey. It looks like the structure grew from the stone.

Once you enter the medieval monastery, to reach the top of the Abbey is rather daunting: the pathway leading to the top is steep, narrow and cobblestoned. There are also many flights of stairs you need to climb. I didn't think I'd be able to make the ascent to the top to see the Abbey church but I did it, along with my family. It was so worth the hike. We were humbled and moved by the feeling in the church; the nuns singing so harmoniously and the mystical beauty surrounding us. Another memory we'll never forget.

After a week spent visiting other sites around our area in Normandy, it was time to fly to our next destination: Prague, the capital of the Czech Republic. I've stayed in Paris, Barcelona, and Venice: the architecture of these cities is magnificent; however, in my mind, Prague truly is unique and stunning. Nicknamed "the City of a Hundred Spires," it's known for its Old Town Square, the heart of its historic core, with colorful baroque buildings.

My father was born not far from Prague so perhaps my genetic roots are stirring. . . I love Prague. And the shops! Oh my—I'll leave that for another day. We also wandered by a unique revolving memorial, a silver statue of the face of Franz Kafka. He was a German-speaking Bohemian novelist and short-story writer, widely regarded as one of the major figures of 20th-century literature. It's so interesting that his stories didn't become widely recognized until after his death. Reminds me of a man called Sydney Banks.

A lovely end to our family vacation. We had 2 wonderful river boat tours on the Vltava River that runs through Prague. One trip was on a large boat that gave us a great look at the magnificent architecture; however, it was hard to hear the audio history so on the spur of the moment, we decided to do a second tour. This tour was on a much smaller craft with a knowledgeable, humorous guide. He was great! He told us fascinating stories of various sites, which included a tour of the Devil's canal, that looks like a mini Venice Canal. Many famous films have been made there, including James Bond movies.

Tomorrow we head for home. All of us are ready; we're feeling perfectly content, filled to the brim with the beauty and joy of our family adventures. Once we arrive home, we'll take time to rest a bit and see what life has in store.

Oh my, how delicious to be home! Our family holiday memories will last forever; a treasure chest of joy and a wealth of new experiences. Having said that about our time away, both Ken and I fell in love with our wee home again. The magic of seeing the familiar with new eyes. First of all, the beautiful park behind the hotel where we stayed the first night in Vancouver, welcomed us back. Then being greeted at our front door by our peonies in full bloom. Heaven on earth.

I'm taking my summer sabbatical; at home, with family and friends. I'm at peace, nestled in our cozy backyard, content to do nothing or everything, whatever moves me in the moment, with Ken by my side or beckoning me to join him for a walk. Enjoy your summer blessings!

Beautiful autumn weather. We love strolling along our harbor boardwalk, walking the trails at Duck Creek park, and Ken in his element, fishing on St. Mary Lake. No matter how much we love our travels around the world, we're always grateful to see the beauty of our island with grateful eyes.

We had the most wonderful family gathering to celebrate Ken's 75th birthday in February, 2019. Ron, our son, and his wife, Lori, joined us, as well as Lynn, and her wife, Kim. We went to Nobu's Japanese Restaurant, Ken's favorite in Victoria.

Elsie Spittle

Ken is looking more handsome and debonair than he was as a teenager when I first met him at the age of 16. I fancied him when I first saw him, in my home room class in high school. Later on, when we started to date, he was such a gentleman, with his English manners, that I was quite taken by this. He was different than the other guys I'd dated.

Ken was born in England, near Leeds, and although he came to Canada as a 4-year-old, his parents retained their accent and mannerisms at home, so Ken grew up with a gentleness about him. Yet, occasionally he was a rebel in school and sometimes at his childhood home. However, he was a "gentle rebel."

Sydney Banks

Syd's Role

Over the years, it's become increasingly important to keep Syd's story at the forefront of our learning, and of the next generation's learning. In my global travels, sharing this precious understanding of the three spiritual gifts Syd uncovered, I was initially surprised when I engaged in conversation with new people interested in the Principles who hadn't heard about Syd.

I discovered when I shared the story of Syd's Enlightenment, and how he began to teach, guided by Mind, that the feeling amongst us grew so deep, and ignited many insights for participants at the retreats I was doing. When I played his early audio tapes and his more current DVDs, people were deeply moved to feel and hear the message directly from the man who uncovered this innate treasure. To have the gift of his original recordings and books is a gift beyond measure.

Syd always said, *"It's the feeling; it's not the words. See beyond the words. If you get a nice feeling, you're getting it."*

It's very important for people to get a sense of how the Principles came into the world, in contemporary times, via the profound revelation of Sydney Banks in 1973. When people see the "genesis" of the Principles, it provides a "big picture" understanding that helps deepen their grounding and strengthens their ability to share what they're learning.

Seeing the big picture also provides a depth of hope for humanity, that an ordinary man, with little education, who wasn't seeking an answer to life, nonetheless, found the gold at the end of the rainbow. The hope this story sparks is that enlightenment and insight can happen to anybody, at any time, whether one knows there is anything deeper in life or not. The hope this story gives is that this innate wisdom and guidance is within "us too."

"The Genesis of the Three Principles—Reflections on the Life and Discoveries of Sydney Banks" is a treasure of a book. It was translated into Spanish from the Genesis DVD, by Ana Holmback and her team. Next, the book was transcribed into English. Ana poured her heart and soul into this creation, as we did when we filmed the original story on Salt Spring Island with Julian Freeman, who is a videographer, devoted to filming and sharing the Three Principles.

Julian did an amazing job of capturing the incredible beauty of the island, and suggested that he film Chip and myself in nature, surrounded by lush greenery, sitting in comfortable chairs on the beach at Ruckle Park. On the film, as we share our observations of Syd's Enlightenment, and the impact his discovery has had on humanity, you can hear the birds and the gentle waves lapping in the background. It's filmed so beautifully. My heart stirs as I recall that special time.

Nuggets of Wisdom II

The film was born from an insight I had while I was doing a retreat in Scotland. I was moved from within to see about bringing Syd's story to life and preserving it for generations to come. I was compelled to honor the miracle that happened to him, never to be forgotten. I shared my insight with Julian in Glasgow and the fire was lit. Long story short, I talked with Ken, and Chip and Jan Chipman; the film became a reality when Julian joined us here on Salt Spring, in July 2015, to help bring our vision to life.

The book has been a collaboration between Ana Holmback and the Three Principles Foundation. All proceeds go directly to the Foundation to disseminate Syd's materials to those in need. I LOVE this book and the DVD! Both are unique and have the power to touch the reader's soul. It's a dream come true, to honor one of the greatest minds of our time; to highlight and cherish Syd's legacy, and to share his gift of the 3 Principles on a global level.

Syd's Message for Humanity

Ken and I knew Syd before he had his Enlightenment and we were with him after his experience. We know that the man was transformed by this experience. It didn't come from reading any spiritual books or from any outside learning. His soul opened and released the wisdom of the ages. There's no way that Syd could have talked at Universities with professors of psychology and psychiatry, had he not had this experience. His epiphany was spontaneous, and it was real. I trust that people's wisdom will discern what's real and what's not.

I'm feeling very moved to be in London to speak at the 3P UK conference, May, 2016. The magic for me started last night, with the international speakers for the conference, gathered together to celebrate Shabbat at Rabbi Rosenblatt and his wife, Chana's, home. At the dinner were people from all different religious backgrounds, in complete alignment, honoring that which is common in all of us; spiritual essence, God. I never thought this kind of gathering would be possible, and I thank Divine providence that gave us Sydney Banks. I know that if the enlightenment Syd experienced hadn't occurred, and Syd hadn't shared his message of the Three Principles, I and the others would not have been sitting at that table.

I had the honor of opening the advanced track of the 3P UK conference. My topic was "The Joy and Value of Continuing Education." I wondered what it would be like to speak with such an enormous crowd of 600 people. I discovered it was just as intimate as if we were gathered in my living room--a very large living room, mind. The crowd felt like my family, so full of love with the feeling of hope and the promise of "now" and the inspiration for tomorrow. The exciting phrase rippling throughout the conference, and the upcoming one in Oslo, is "One Solution to all Problems." Syd predicted this at the very beginning of his teachings. Apparently, the time has come!

It's extraordinary to see how Sydney Banks' message is being recognized around the world. Truly, an inner evolution is taking place. A year ago today, May 26th, 2015, I had the privilege of being on a panel invited to speak on how to promote well-being, at an event held at Scotland's Parliament, sponsored by Jacquie Forde. This evening, I had the pleasure of being in the audience of the One Solution conference in Oslo, hearing the amazing speakers addressing global concerns. United Nations representatives are part of this conference. Sydney Banks vision of the Three Principles alleviating humanity's suffering is taking a giant leap. I feel it's rather significant that both these historic events happened on the same day, one year apart. I'm very moved by this.

When I first heard Syd use the word "God" in his talks, I found this very confusing. Based on my religious upbringing, I had always thought that God was an entity. I also was aware that Syd did not consider himself a religious man, so I wondered why he was talking about God, when he never had before his experience. After his epiphany, he called himself "a spiritual man."

When I asked him why he seemed to distinguish between what I understood, that God was an entity, and how he spoke of God, he said, *"I'm talking about God as pure spiritual energy. I'm talking about Divine Mind, Master Mind, Innate Wisdom, that spiritual energy that is within us all."* Although I still didn't understand what he meant, I "felt" the truth of this. This feeling was very helpful to me. It calmed my intellect so that I could just rest in "not knowing."

Nuggets of Wisdom II

When Syd talked to us in the early days about submitting to God's will, he made it clear that he meant *"submitting to our innate spiritual wisdom."* He wasn't talking about submitting to an "entity." He always pointed us back to our own spiritual intelligent essence.

Sydney Banks said at the beginning of his teaching that opting out of the world to find peace wasn't the answer. Some of his earliest students, including me and my husband, left society because we were disillusioned and thought we would find peace by "going back to the land." This is what he told us, *"You are society. Change yourself and the world will change."*

I was the typist for Syd when he wrote *"Second Chance."* Often times, he would hand me an assortment of papers to transcribe. Some sentences might be written on napkins, if he had been in a cafe and an insight came to him. He used whatever materials were available. I loved his words; whatever form they came in to me! One of my favorite Syd quotes: *"True philosophy has no rules, regulations, or rituals holding it prisoner. It's as free as the trade winds."*

Elsie Spittle

I remember a talk Syd gave in the very early days at a Church in the United States, just before Easter. He had been invited by a woman minister, which in itself, in those days, was highly unusual. Ken and I were in the audience and were really taken by what he said about Passover, as he'd never ever said anything about this before. He said *"Passover is like passing from the outside world to the inside world, from the form to the formless."* To this day, the words resonate so deeply within me.

⁓

When Syd told me this, *"You must realize that the negative feelings and emotions from past traumatic experiences are no longer true. They are merely memories, a collection of old, stale thoughts,"* I found freedom from my past trauma, from situations that I had previously thought impossible to forget. I still remember them occasionally, but without the pain those thoughts used to cause me.

⁓

This is the first year, 2018, I've not been a speaker at the 3P UK conference, due to conflicting dates with a preplanned family vacation. I will miss seeing all my friends, new ones and familiar faces. The spiritual space that arises when so many are gathered to honor the universal essence of our True Nature is beyond description. I will miss that most of all.

Nuggets of Wisdom II

However, I am finding a special blossoming of family relations on our vacation, and after all is said and done, that's really what Sydney Bank's message of the Three Principles offers. Enjoyment of the everyday moments and miracles.

I send my love to all the presenters. I know you all offer a unique, distinct voice based on your own wisdom. To the audience, you are in for an unforgettable event that has the power to transform your lives. Together, you bear witness to a miracle that happened to an ordinary man over four decades ago, a miracle that continues to manifest throughout the world, simply by each of us living more fully in our core essence.

May 25, 2019. I'm in London and feeling nostalgic. It's a decade today since Sydney Banks went "home." On one hand, I feel incredibly grateful to have journeyed with an Enlightened being. On the other hand, I miss him. I know I wouldn't be in London, about to present at my last 3P UK Conference, if it weren't for Syd's message rippling out into the world, helping to alleviate human suffering. The conference with 1,000 people in attendance wouldn't be happening, if not for Syd. This humble working man gave such an extraordinary gift to the world—3 spiritual gifts underlying all human experience. My heart is full of love.

The Gift of the Unknown

The Gift of the Unknown

A poignant moment, waiting to say "goodbye " to a thousand people at my last talk at the 3P UK Conference, June 2019. Now, a new chapter begins in my life. I don't know what the next chapter holds. I just know that it will be beautiful.

Rabbi Shaul gave me a heartfelt introduction before my last talk, letting people know this would be my last conference. The audience groaned in dismay. . . I raised my hands in glee and loudly proclaimed "Yay," knowing that my life was about to become simpler and richer in learning. "Knowing" provides comfort and patience when one is unsure of what comes next, and that knowing is enough. That knowing is our true nature holding us steady during change.

When we come to a crossroads in life, we may struggle with knowing what we want to do next. It was a big insight for me to realize that it was enough to know what I didn't want to do. This gave me mental space to relax and wait for the next step forward to manifest.

Elsie Spittle

When we acknowledge what we don't want to do, the space that frees up in our mind allows fresh insights to come forth, guiding us forward to the next phase of our life.

～～⌒⌒

You don't have to stick with something that no longer feels right. It's not a sign of weak will. For example, I'd finished an online mentoring program and although I loved it, I wasn't sure if I wanted to do another in the same format. I rested in not knowing. Then it came to me; insight for another, shorter version that was alive with energy. I knew without question that this is what I was meant to do, at that moment in time. Mind then provided more insights on the format, topics, time, all practical and at the same time profound. I love how we are all mentored by Mind.

～～⌒⌒

"Hope" used to be a nebulous concept to me until I had my first insight. I learned to "just live" as best I could. I simply felt hopeful because I was enjoying my life. My enjoyment of life wasn't conditional. I didn't have anything on it. I wasn't bargaining with myself, that if I stayed hopeful, life would be good. I trusted that being in the moment, living life in gratitude, is hope in action.

Epilogue

Epilogue

We've come to the end of the book, not to the end of the journey. That's one of the gifts I love about this understanding. Our inner journey never ends. Our souls will continue to evolve. Every soul on this planet has a purpose; sometimes not understood. In my heart, I feel our primary purpose is to love the world and everything in it unconditionally. To be kind to one another; to honor the essence within each of us; occasionally, despite the outward behavior.

Thank you for reading my offerings. My hope is that a nugget or two may have sparked something within you that is new and fresh, that enlightens your journey.

I'll end with one of my favorite Sydney Banks' quotes: *"You don't have to understand the Principles in order to benefit from them."*

Further Reading

Genesis of the Three Principles: Reflections on the Life and Discoveries of Sydney Banks is now available.

https://www.amazon.com/dp/1702631303

Syd's website archived. www.sydneybanks.org

Link for Books, Audios and Videos by Sydney Banks:

http://sydbanks.com/

More digital and books of Sydney Banks can be found here:

https://books.apple.com/us/author/sydney-banks/id1141097963

Resources

3 Principles for Human Development (Elsie's website)

www.3phd.net

Three Principles Foundation (hosts the School on Salt Spring Island)

www.threeprinciplesfoundation.org

Your own wisdom!

Acknowledgements

It's been an absolute pleasure working on this book with my daughter, Lynn Spittle, and her wife, Kim Patriquin. The invitation to work with them was born from an insight I had. Their acceptance was immediate, flavored with excitement and a tiny bit of insecurity that vanished as we delved into the raw material of my manuscript. As they organized the material, questions arose from them that prompted insightful conversations between the three of us.

Both listened deeply to my suggestions for the format and layout of the book and cover and brought back ideas that were better than mine. Lynn redesigned the original cover of the first Nuggets of Wisdom book with endless patience and many samples until I was completely satisfied. I'm so very grateful for their loving and brilliant assistance.

Special thanks to Ken, for his excellent eye, in helping choose the finished product, and for listening to and taking part in countless discussions about the text and design.

So much gratitude to Jane Tucker who has never hesitated to help me by adding the final editorial polish to this manuscript, as well as all my other books.

Printed in Great Britain
by Amazon

47489394R00115